# THEN Isaac SOWED

APOSTLE LYNROY C. SCANTLEBURY

Copyright © 2024 by Apostle Lynroy C. Scantlebury

Paperback: 978-1-965632-92-5
eBook: 978-1-965632-93-2
Library of Congress Control Number: 2024925870

All rights reserved. No part of this publication may be reproduced, distributed, or transmitted in any form or by any electronic or mechanical means, without the prior written permission of the publisher, except in the case of brief quotations embodied in critical reviews and certain other noncommercial uses permitted by copyright law.

This Book is a work of fiction. Names, characters, places, and incidents either are the product of the author's imagination or are used fictitiously. Any resemblance to actual persons, living or dead, events, or locales is entirely coincidental.

Ordering Information:

Prime Seven Media
518 Landmann St.
Tomah City, WI 54660

Printed in the United States of America

# TABLE OF CONTENTS

# INTRODUCTION

As a Minister in the body of Christ, it is never easy when we are corrected about having preached or taught a passage of scripture incorrectly. What you are about to read in this book is about such a correction that was given to me as a result of a divine visitation from the Angel of the Lord who came to me for seven consecutive nights.

What I received during those seven nights was truly an eye-opening and life changing experience in understanding the word of God at a new level, and also how misunderstanding and misinterpretation of it can deny it of its true power to produce results in our lives on a consistent basis.

During this visitation, the Angel explained the reason for his presence at this time, and the role that I was required to play to assist in bringing about the correction that the body of Christ is to experience now.

I knew that my life was about to be changed forever as I listened attentively to the Angel's explanation of the current error that was being preached and taught in the body of

Christ today, the damage it was causing, and the subsequent implementation of the corrective measures that will be taken by the Kingdom of God to reposition the body of Christ on the original path to the dominion it should have in the earth realm.

His visitation, as explained as the restoring of the precise reality of the text surrounding the error, so that the true understanding of it would aid the Father in reinstating a new dimension of results and financial excellence in the Body of Christ worldwide.

I was also made aware of the doors within the body of Christ that were opened to satanic forces through this error, and the creation of increase poverty and failure that has plagued many as a result of it.

The importance and urgency of this correction at this time was made abundantly clear to me and I became quite numb as the Angel he said, "if spiritual principles are applied under incorrect preaching of the word of God, the spiritual principle will not work and the expected result will fail, and God cannot be forced to operate against his laws". He further explained spiritual laws are as much a seed as the word of God is, but the word also acts as the ground for the spiritual principle. If the spiritual principle is sown into a word or instruction that isn't fertile the seed of that spiritual principle will die.

The Angel said that this constitutes a dimension of robbery in the Body of Christ. The individual applying the spiritual principle is robbed of resources and results, and God is robbed through not being able to cause power to be released to bring about the return. It was explained that when there is an acute dimension of robbery in the Body of Christ and also in the world economic system, it allows satanic forces to create economic instability in nations thus creating poverty and hardship, which becomes agents of failure and death.

It was then share with me that my assignment that through this book a divine consciousness that was given to Isaac through the experience that he had during his time in Gerar, will be again be released into the body of Christ.

This consciousness must be received as a higher level gift to the Body of Christ through leaders who are ready to operate with the same mind in achieving a spiritual power that overcomes the limitations of the earth realm, and assisting members of the body of Christ and individuals in the world to understand God's desire to bless humanity in amazing ways,

I pray that as you read, you will sense the presence and power I experience during this visitation, and that the hundredfold will manifest in your life.

Apostle Lynroy C. Scantlebury

CHAPTER ONE

# UNDERSTANDING ISAAC'S HUNDREDFOLD MANIFESTATION

After our initial introduction, the Angel began to draw my attention to the Genesis chapter 26, and asked me to read it. As I did so the Angel said, "I will now reveal to you why I have been sent and what I must make known to you at this time to open the door of a new higher consciousness that will produce a quick turning of financial overflow and abundance in the Body of Christ".

He began shared with me that within this biblical passage a great and mighty act took place, but however the revelation it has been blocked, through a widespread misunderstanding of the passage.

He continued to explain that this text is widely used in Christian teaching and preaching to disseminate the knowledge of

Isaac receiving the hundredfold increase from God in the same year. However the power of this hundredfold increase potential has been marred by the incorrect implication that Isaac was able to receive this mighty achievement during a time of famine.

The angel revealed to me that this implication of Isaac sowing in the time of famine was due to the combining of Genesis 26.1 and Genesis 26:12.

**Gen 26:1**

**1** AND THERE was a famine in the land, other than the former famine that was in the days of Abraham. And Isaac went to Gerar, to Abimelech king of the Philistines. AMP

**Gen 26:12**

**12** Then Isaac sowed seed in that land and received in the same year a hundred times as much as he had planted, and the Lord favored him with blessings. AMP

The combination of these two verses of the text by teaches and preachers, created the idea in the minds of the hearers that Isaac highly blessed of the Lord that was able to supernaturally overcome a negative climatic phenomenon and place seed into famine affected soil and was still able to see the hundredfold increase in his seed. This however isn't the case, ISAAC DID NOT SOW DURING A TIME OF FAMINE.

In fact for Isaac to achieve the Hundredfold increase in his agricultural experience, God would have to break his law of Seedtime and Harvest, Genesis 8:22 and seed being sown into good ground, Mathew 13:8.

During the season when the concept of Isaac sowing in the time of famine and reaping the hundredfold in the same year was being taught and preached in the Body of Christ worldwide, much money was moved and given with the expectation of the hundredfold increase manifesting, but many were left disappointed. This activity affected what the kingdom of God was attempting to implement during many season of Spiritual transitions in the Body of Christ.

The reason for this is due to the combination of several errors which includes...

1. The Incorrect Revelation of the text.
2. Incorrect Consciousness and Principle in Sowing.
3. Misunderstanding the process of the Hundredfold Manifestation.

Once persons were responded to a request to sow or give money with the mind-set of receiving a hundredfold increase base on Isaac sowing in the time of famine, it instantly becomes an act of error in the divine principle. The angel said to me, "I will now go through this passage with you and show you the secrets of how this hundredfold Increase actually came about and I will even show you more that you may reveal to those your minister too and who I will direct to read this book."

## POINT: DON'T BE AFRAID TO MAKE ADJUSTMENTS.

### Gen 26:1 AMP

**1** AND THERE was a famine in the land, other than the former famine that was in the days of Abraham. And Isaac went to Gerar, to Abimelech king of the Philistines.

If you noticed that in the first verse of Genesis 26, it is clear to see that Isaac was moving away from the famine. He made a decision to seek betterment for his family by seeking other countries that weren't being affected by the famine that was in his country. With a wife and two sons, It would not have made any sense for him to stay where the famine was at all. The fact that Isaac had journeyed to another country instantly rules out the concept that he sowed seed in famished ground, because he was not where the famine was.

It is important to note here that the scripture refers to a famine and not a drought. Famine can be due to crop failure or overpopulation. Crop failure in the bible isn't due only to a lack of rainfall; it can also be the result of pest infestation or war.

The word means: Extreme and general scarcity of food, as in a country or large geographical area; a severe shortage of food through crop failure or overpopulation Any extreme and general scarcity; acute shortage of anything, Extreme hunger; starvation.

The Angel said to me, "if you notice clearly, Isaac was moving in a specific way for he went to Abimelech who was the king of the Phillistine city of Gerar." The angel went on to explain here that many in the body of Christ choose to stay in the famine because of fear of uncertainty and failure. Many are awaiting some special sign from God in order to be certain that the time to move has come, but the child of God should be knowledgeable enough to conscious of the steps that leads to progressive success and prosperity on larger scales.

Many people choose to stay where the famine is and expect to see God move on their behalf, and when they see no results, they blame the devil or decide that maybe it is not God's will for this or that to happen. They continue to work jobs that are unfulfilling, mentally stimulating, without opportunities for advancement and financially rewarding. They seldom take advantage of courses and opportunities in the educational arena that will position for increases and promotion. They become callous as it regards investing and planning for a better life. This also applies to them continuing to sit in churches and ministries with leaders who are no longer operating with the kingdom of God and its assignment for this new season.

## POINT: HAVING A HIGH-RANKING FAMILY FRIEND

The Angel had me to focus on this aspect of the first verse; Isaac went to Abimelech King of the Phillistine in Gerar. He told me that this is a vital key in the events that led up to Isaac's achieving the hundredfold increase.

This is the first stop of Isaac in his journey away from his home land and the famine. He came to a family friend of his father Abraham named King Abimelech. However Isaac only planned for this visit to be brief since his true intent was to go to Egypt.

### Gen 26:2 AMP

And the Lord appeared to him and said, <u>Do not go down to Egypt</u>; live in the land of which I will tell you.

The Angel then directed me to pay a closer look at the Philistine King Abimelech and his city Gerar. His name means, Father of the King, and Gerar means pilgrimage, combat and dispute. King Abimelech comes into the sequence of events during the life of Isaac's father Abraham.

Based on the account of Genesis Chapter 20, a situation occurs where Abraham is moving from his homeland due to a famine, and makes a stop in Gerar. During the time he was there, Abraham made it known that Sarah his wife was his sister, and this act made King Abimelech send his servants to bring her to the palace to become one of his concubines.

According to the text God appeared to King Abimelech in a vision and told him that he was to restore Sarah to Abraham, because she was actually his wife. God also had cause a high increase in barrenness among the King's servants so that they couldn't become pregnant.

The account continues with God telling King Abimelech that Abraham was a Prophet and that he would pray for him and his household so that they could conceive and bear children. King Abimelech invited Abraham to pray and God opened their wombs.

This encounter led to King Abimelech being very favourable the both Abraham and Sarah.

The second account with King Abimelech is recorded in Genesis chapter 21. This is some years after Isaac was born and had actually grown into a strong youth. Here King Abimelech visits Abraham to make a covenant with him because he recognised that Abraham's God is with him and causing him to prosper in all that he was doing.

### Gen 21:22-24 AMP

**22** At that time Abimelech and Phicol the commander of his army said to Abraham, God is with you in everything you do.

**23** So now, swear to me here by God that you will not deal falsely with me or with my son or with my posterity; but as I have dealt with you kindly, you will do the same with me and with the land in which you have sojourned.

**24** And Abraham said, I will swear.

This is incredible, King Abimelech asked Abraham to enter into an agreement to protect him and his descendants and to deal kindly with them. This covenant really placed Abraham in a very powerful position and he agreed to it.

When do we hear that rulers of nations, Governors, Presidents, Prime Minister, Mayors, ask Men and Women of God not to deal with them falsely?

The second account involving King Abimelech and Abraham is recorded in Genesis 21 as well.

### Gen 21:30-32 AMP

**30** He said, You are to accept these seven ewe lambs from me as a witness for me that I dug this well.

**31** Therefore that place was called Beersheba [well of the oath], because there both parties swore an oath.

**32** Thus they made a covenant at Beersheba; then Abimelech and Phicol the commander of his army returned to the land of the Philistines.

In this case Abraham had dug a well that was seized by some of King Abimelech's servants, and Abraham complained to Abimelech about it. So they entered into an agreement that would protect Abraham and any well that he dug.

After being enlightened to the reality of this royal friendship between Abraham and Abimelech, the Angel said, "Do you see that Isaac wasn't going to a stranger when he went to King Abimelech? Isaac went to a family friend, a very powerful and wealthy family friend."

The Angel went on to explain to me the power of the covenant between Abraham and Abimelech. He said, "This is a covenant between two fathers, one being the Father of a Multitude (Abraham) and the other being the Father of the King (Abimelech)."

He continued to reveal that the lack of individuals and believes seeking to apply the principle of having wealthy and influential people in their lives is at a very low operational level. He also shared with me that many Christians believe that all their friends must be Christians, and that it isn't right to create relationships with wealth persons. Many indivduals and believers experience seasons of stagnation due to not having influential people that they can turn to in their lives. They have found themselves in a position where they have to face this current crisis alone, without the aid or support of people who have the resources and ability to make things happen for them. Many times we are way too traditional and do not seem to know how to harness the fine lines of relationship in life, business and the Kingdom, and how to perfectly balance them in such a way to maintain harmony and achieving maximum benefit. Some individuals seem to the idea that God will supernaturally materialize everything we need from, but we have to understand that God provides through people. God has a way of speaking to people about us. Sometimes He speaks to people we don't expect Him to, but we have to learn the ways of God.

The Angel started to show me how this principle was employed in the bible by individuals such as King David.

**1 Samuel 22:3 AMP**

**3** And David went from there to Mizpah of Moab; and he said to the king of Moab, Let my father [of Moabite descent] and my mother, I pray you, come out [of Judah] and be with you till I know what God will do for me.

During the season of running from King Saul, David employed the Principle of having an Influential family friend, when he took his mother and father to the King of Moab, and asked him to take care of them until he became more aware of the will of God for his life.

The Angel also showed me how King Solomon applied the principle in his own life.

## 2 Chronicles 2:3 AMP

**3** And Solomon sent to Hiram king of Tyre, saying, As you dealt with David my father and sent him cedars to build himself a house in which to dwell, even so deal with me.

Solomon's father King David had a very powerful and wealthy Royal friend named King Hiram of Tyre. This King loved David and even sent him all the timber and workmen to build him a house.

After King David died, Solomon who was immensely rich due to the inheritance that his father left him wrote King Hiram a letter asking him to extend the favor he showed to King David to him. You may say that with all the wisdom and wealth Solomon had, why ask King Hiram for help. Remember Solomon was wise. It shows that this principle is not just for persons without financial resources it works for anyone who will put it to work.

In addition to this, the Angel showed me aspects of Jesus's life and ministry where he applied this principle.

## Luke 16:9

**9** And I tell you, make friends for yourselves by means of unrighteous mammon (deceitful riches, money, possessions), so that when it fails, they [those you have favored] may receive and welcome you into the everlasting habitations (dwellings).

**Luke 8:2-3**

**2** And also some women who had been cured of evil spirits and diseases: Mary called Magdalene, from whom seven demons had been expelled;

**3** And Joanna, the wife of Chuza, Herod's household manager; and Susanna; and many others, who ministered to and provided for i Him and them out of their property and personal belongings.

Jesus himself had people that supported his ministry and disciples; he was not some nomadic loner walking around begging or saying "I'm just trusting the Lord to meet my need." He made connections out of his ministry. Just think of the countless numbers of lives that were changed and helped simply because of a connection to wealthy or influential individuals. This principle calls for decisive action on the part of one seeking for a better and more proactive way of living. Do not sit on the side lines any longer, get up and get involved. They are influential individuals in your country and all over the world that are capable of creating leverage, granting opportunity and opening doors for you in life faster than you can imagine. Apply this principle to your life today and release your faith to the Lord to connect you with an influential individual.

CHAPTER 2

# ALLOW THE LORD TO CHANGE YOUR PLANS

The Angel continued to open my eyes to the hidden truths in the text of Genesis Chapter 26. At this point he showed me how Isaac received direct instructions from the Lord regarding his initial plan of going to Egypt. The Lord asked him not to go down to Egypt.

**Gen 26:2 AMP**

**2** And the Lord appeared to him and said, Do not go down to Egypt; live in the land of which I will tell you.

He explained to me that the Lord asked Isaac to stay in Gerar with King Abimelech. Remember that Gerar means pilgrimage, combat and dispute. Knowing this, Isaac certainly wouldn't have easily received this as a sensible instruction form the Lord. No one would want to stay in a place of combat and dispute, but, as the Angel said, "The instructions of the Lord are never without his highest desire for the one receiving the instructions."

We have to easily allow the Holy Spirit to change our mind many times on the spot, and allow the divine to intercept us at strategic times and seasons. The Angel explained of the hardest things for the Lord to do in the lives of believers is to get them to change their minds. To many everything has to make sense to them before they believe or act on an instruction from the Lord. The man or woman who finds it difficult to change his or her mind and wants to obey the promptings and commands of the Lord will continue in a constant downward spiral in this life. This principle is going to be very critical in this season. Maybe you are planning to relocate, start a new business, buy a new house or vehicle, study for a career change or even launch a ministry. Take the time out to listen to the voice of the Lord. He may want you to change your mind and follow His leading. Remember, the Lord knows best for our lives. Success and prosperity come from Him.

**Prov 3:5-6 AMP says,**

**5** Lean on, trust in, and be confident in the Lord with all your heart and mind and do not rely on your own insight or understanding.

**6** In all your ways know, recognize, and acknowledge Him, and He will direct and make straight and plain your paths.

Isaac did obey the instruction of the Lord, and settled in Gerar. However we must look at the promises of the Lord that came along with the instruction. As we will see, the Lord gave Isaac detailed promises as to why he should stay in Gerar and the promises were convincing enough to cause him to act instantly.

**Gen 26:3-4AMP**

**3** Dwell temporarily in this land, and I will be with you and will favor you with blessings; for to you and to your descendants I will give all these lands, and I will perform the oath which I swore to Abraham your father.

**4** And I will make your descendants to multiply as the stars of the heavens, and will give to your posterity all these lands (kingdoms); and by your Offspring shall all the nations of the earth be blessed, or by Him bless themselves,

## POINT: UNDERSTANDING THE PROMISES AND THE PERFORMANCE OF THE OATH OF ABRAHAM

As I listened attentively to the Angel my mind began to open up to the reality that without the aid of the Spirit, the bible is just word. As we took a closer look at vs. 3 and 4 of the text, the Lord makes several lavish promises to Isaac, and this is where the Angel took me through a thorough assessment of each promise so that I could actual feel the power behind him convincing Isaac to stay in Gerar and what he planned to manifest in Isaac's life during that season. Let's see what they are really revealing:

1. I will be with you = Divine presence
2. I will favor you with blessings = Uncommon power for results
3. I will give you and your descendants ALL these lands = Divine ownership transfer
4. I will perform the oath which I swore to Abraham = I'm going to do in your life what I agreed with Abraham.
5. And I will make your descendants to multiply as the stars of the heavens = Exponential Increase.
6. By your Offspring shall all the nations of the earth be blessed = Worldwide Blessing Manifestation.

All of these promises the Lord told Isaac he will do while he is Gerar. Through these promises, the Lord raised Isaac's expectations and conditioned his mind to believe for the manifestation of these promises. He was going to cause Isaac to experience a level of divine activity that he never saw before, even in a place of combat and dispute. Isaac could actually look forward to the fulfilment of these promises in a place where it normally would be uncommon for a stranger to have this level of success and prosperity manifested.

The Angel specifically drew my attention to the fourth thing the Lord said to Isaac, said that this was the vital element. He said "The Lord told Isaac that he will perform the oath that he swore to his father Abraham." In other words Isaac becomes the first person to actually benefit from the manifestation of this oath.

To fully understand the magnitude of the oath of Abraham, we have to take a look at the actual text which is recorded in Genesis 22:15-18.

### Gen 22:15-18 AMP

The Angel of the Lord called to Abraham from heaven a second time,

**16** And said, I have sworn by Myself, says the Lord, that since you have done this and have not withheld [from Me] or begrudged [giving Me] your son, your only son,

**17** In blessing I will bless you and in multiplying I will multiply your descendants like the stars of the heavens and like the sand on the seashore. And your Seed (Heir) will possess the gate of His enemies,

**18** And in your Seed [w Christ] shall all the nations of the earth be blessed and [by Him] bless themselves, because you have heard and obeyed My voice.

In this account, Abraham is about to actually sacrifice Isaac to the Lord as a burnt offering, when he was stopped by the Angel of the Lord. The text explains how the Lord spoke to Abraham and outlined to him the divine plan for his descendants.

As I continue to revolve the text in my mind, the Angel asked. "What do you see?" my reply to the question was simply that I see the Lord increasing Abraham's descendants, granting them victory over the enemy and blessing the world. The Angel said, "Very good, but now let me show you what is hidden." He said "What is hidden is the secret to all hundredfold manifestation, and that secret is the possessing of the gates of your enemies. This is the Divine War, this is what the Lord promised Abraham and it is what he also promised Isaac as an expected manifestation during his time in Gerar."

The Angel said that the gates here are the earthly rulers who are actual channels for higher satanic forces to operate through, and based on their beliefs, traditions and operations the gate can remain open in nations and territories for year, and become blockages and hindrances to moves of the kingdom of God.

In continuing his explanation, the Angel said that even though Abimelech was such a ruler, and presided over the place of combat and dispute (Gerar), no one like Isaac ever visited his city, so the possessing of the gates of the enemy couldn't be enforced. The point is that it takes Abraham's seed to visit, not just anyone.

## Gal 3:29AMP

**29** And if you belong to Christ [are in Him Who is Abraham's Seed], then you are Abraham's offspring and [spiritual] heirs according to promise.

Based on the word of God, you and I are Abrahams seed and therefore we are entitled the having this powerful oath manifested on our lives.

Isaac was going to benefit from this oath that guaranteed him a Divine attack on the human and satanic forces that were controlling the gates within and over Gerar.

The Angel explained to me that this was the perfect setup by the Lord with Isaac positioned in Gerar, because this will be the first time that such a divine attempt would be made in the life of a human being, so it's clear to see that Isaac was set for the hundredfold increase long before he even sowed any seed.

He continued explaining that the same principle is used by Jesus in the construction of his church.

## Matt 16:18 AMP

**18** And I tell you, you are Peter [Greek, Petros — a large piece of rock], and on this rock [Greek, petra — a huge rock like Gibraltar] I will build My church, and the gates of Hades (the powers of the infernal region) shall not overpower it [or be strong to its detriment or hold out against it].

Jesus enforced the oath of Abraham as a resultant state of the church. His church will be in control of the gates of the enemy. His church will benefit from the Divine War, an actual attack on enemy forces through the church to possess them.

He went on to share a deeper understanding of the text in Matt 16:18, stating that once the revelation of Jesus being the Christ came from the Father through a human being, it meant that certain strategic and unchangeable promises could now be claimed by Jesus as the Christ. When Jesus Christ made the decision to select the promises, he selected the promises of God that carried the most weight, were more binding, powerful and unchangeable.

Spiritually speaking, it must be understood that the promises God made with Abraham were really with himself and Christ. Notice as the Apostle Paul reveals the truth of what really occurred.

### Gal 3:16 AMP

**16** Now the promises (covenants, agreements) were decreed and made to Abraham and his Seed (his Offspring, his Heir). He [God] does not say, And to seeds (descendants, heirs), as if referring to many persons, but, And to your Seed (your

Descendant, your Heir), obviously referring to one individual, Who is [none other than] Christ (the Messiah).

### Heb 6:12 AMP

**13** For when God made [His] promise to Abraham, He swore by Himself, since He had no one greater by whom to swear.

### Heb 6:16-18 AMP

**16** Men indeed swear by a greater [than themselves], and with them in all disputes the oath taken for confirmation is final [ending strife].

**17** Accordingly God also, in His desire to show more convincingly and beyond doubt to those who were to inherit the promise the unchangeableness of His purpose and plan, intervened (mediated) with an oath.

**18** This was so that, by two unchangeable things [His promise and His oath] in which it is impossible for God ever to prove false or deceive us, we who have fled [to Him] for refuge might have mighty indwelling strength and strong encouragement to grasp and hold fast the hope appointed for us and set before [us].

The Apostle Paul reveals that when God made promise to Abraham, he swore by himself, and since Christ is the Son of God and is a part of the Godhead, then the promises were made to him. Once Christ was manifested on the earth, he had the legal right to claim and enforce these promises.

**Gal 3:27 AMP**

**27** For as many [of you] as were baptized into Christ [into a spiritual union and communion with Christ, the Anointed One, the Messiah] have put on (clothed yourselves with) Christ.

This reveals a very important principle to every child of God. As one baptized into Christ, we have clothed ourselves with Christ. Therefore on a superlative level we are Christ, and this gives us the right to claim the promise of possessing the gates of our enemies.

As a final point of revelation, the Angel said, "I will now show you the root of the real hundredfold increase." He then directed my attention to Romans Chapter 4:13.

**Rom 4:13 AMP**

**13** For the promise to Abraham or his posterity, that he should inherit the world, did not come through [observing the commands of] the Law but through the righteousness of faith.

The Angel said to me that the root of all hundredfold increase is hidden in this verse. He said that Abraham and his descendants were promised the world as an inheritance, and therefore, if you inherit the world, then that itself is a hundredfold increase and as principle, The Lord will give you any lower manifestation of the hundredfold increase if we truly claim it and believe that we will receive it in this life.

It is not the Church that is destined to be defeated by the enemy; it is the enemy's destiny to be defeated by the Church (Christ's Body). These four principles are going to be the keys to jump-start your belief system for swift change and divine momentum as we move out of the current recession. If you are willing to believe these principles and apply them to your life in obedience to the Lord, then you will begin to see the God of Isaac manifested in your life. Let us examine vs. 4 and receive what the Lord said as he continued his promises to Isaac:

**Gen 26:4**

And I will make your descendants to multiply as the stars of the heavens, and will give to your posterity all these lands (kingdoms); and by your Offspring shall all the nations of the earth be blessed, or by Him bless themselves.

As I read this verse the Lord spoke to me and said 'write this as I want you to':

1. I will make your descendants to multiply as the stars of the heavens = The Body of Christ in increase exponentially in the

earth 2. I will give to your posterity all these lands (kingdoms) = The Body of Christ will have dominion in the earth 3. All the nations of the earth be blessed, or by Him bless themselves = Jesus Christ will be revealed to the world as the blesser by His body in the earth

From this verse, the Lord shared with me that one of the problems that was created during the season of the message of financial prosperity is that many ministers and believers became so incensed on becoming wealthy that they completely forgot the real reason for the message. God said to me: "I wanted the people wealthy so they could bless the world, but now greed has set in, excessive luxury and wantonness has enveloped many in the pulpit and the pew. The adversary has gotten in and redirected my people. Now I am here to reinstate my original plan and purpose, and set the Body of Christ on course again."

What is revealed in these verses are the divine belief system and the original divine purpose. These, as the Lord revealed to me, must come once more into the consciousness of believers worldwide. We must begin to really believe the revelation of the promises of the Lord and do His original will again.

This is a good opportunity to assess ourselves and see if we really believe the Lord and His promises. We must also critically assess if we are attached to ministries and ministers who are really seeking to bless the world. These are going to be vitally important in the lives of believers, because we can no longer play the game of just going to any church or ministry. We must be careful where we choose to plant ourselves or we can end up wasting years and precious resources.

God simply wants us to trust Him and do his will. That is the principle that our forefathers lived by in the Bible; not seven, ten or twelve steps to the best life, just trust, reliance, adherence to and belief in God and doing His will.

Will you be one of those who will hear God's voice today and simply begin to trust and obey Him?

CHAPTER 3

# SPIRITUAL LINEAGE IS IMPORTANT

In this chapter the Angel began to speak to me about the importance of having Godly biological and spiritual lineage. He emphasised the point of how the Lord was able to testify to Isaac about the extent of Abraham's level of obedience and depth of relationship with Him.

He said, "What we see here is the truth that the Lord had decided to enrich Isaac's life because of his ancestry and not through some act of his own, for it's the resultant state of Abraham's life with the Lord that is producing the Divine Visitation that Isaac is experiencing."

**Gen 26:5-6**

**5** For Abraham listened to and obeyed My voice and kept My charge, My commands, My statutes, and My laws.

**6** So Isaac stayed in Gerar. AMP

The Angel explained that this was the key to convincing Isaac to stay in Gerar. It was a challenge from the Lord to Isaac to begin the practice of obeying the voice of the Lord, keeping His charges, commands, statutes and laws just like his father Abraham did.

"You see Lynroy, most individuals don't know how important spiritual lineage is to God and his divine system of continuity. Even in the Body of Christ, many loathe the concept of spiritual father and mothers, and operate as loaners ministerially not knowing that his opens the door for satanic forces to create stagnation and prevent them from moving into higher dimensions and levels."

I asked the Angel to tell me the truth about the reality of having spiritual fathers and mothers and the revelation behind it. He then directed me to Exodus Chapter 3 verses 14-15.

**Ex 3:14-15AMP**

**14** And God said to Moses, I AM WHO I AM and WHAT I AM, and I WILL BE WHAT I WILL BE; and He said, You shall say this to the Israelites: I AM has sent me to you!

**15** God said also to Moses, This shall you say to the Israelites: The Lord, the God of your fathers, of Abraham, of Isaac, and of Jacob, has sent me to you! This is My name forever, and by this name I am to be remembered to all generations. AMP

As I listened intently to receive this very critical information, the Angel asked, "Do you see it? Do you see how in the calling of Moses how the Lord firstly reveals his own name and secondly those with whom his name is connected to? He told Moses that he was the God of his Fathers and this is His name for ever, the God of Abraham, Isaac and Jacob."

He then explain that spiritual fatherhood and motherhood isn't just about having someone with a large ministry that you associate yourself with as a spiritual son or daughter, or someone who has been in ministry for many years, but it is about the wither the individual has been coded into the name of God through extraordinary relationship with God.

The Angel explained that spiritual parents must be evolutionists or pioneers and must be seeking to pass on to the next generation the greater plan for greater promise fulfilment and manifestation.

### Heb 11:16 AMP

**16** But the truth is that they were yearning for and aspiring to a better and more desirable country, that is, a heavenly [one]. For that reason God is not ashamed to be called their God [even to be surnamed their God – the God of Abraham, Isaac, and Jacob], for He has prepared a city for them.

He said, "if you look at this verse closely, you will see that Abraham, Isaac and Jacob were evolutionists and pioneers, it reveals that they were seekers of the Higher manifestations that completely controlled the natural realms, to the point that God connected his name to theirs and actually built them the Heavenly City they desired."

As the angel continued to share this mind blowing concept of spiritual parentage and lineage, I could only thank God for my personal connection to Dr. Oral Roberts. This revelation completely revolutionized my thinking in this regards and how necessary it is for children of God to be connected properly to true spiritual parents.

Being divinely connected to a man or woman of God that hears and obeys the voice of God, a person who knows and walks in the way of the Lord and keeps His laws and commandments, and is an evolutionist and pioneer in spiritual things is going to be another vital principle for all of us who will see more manifestation from God in this time.

The Lord clearly stated to Isaac that he had a strong spiritual heritage. His father had a track record of obeying the Lord. Our spiritual connection and or association are very important to God.

## 2 Kings 2:11-14 AMP

**11** As they still went on and talked, behold, a chariot of fire and horses of fire parted the two of them, and Elijah went up by a whirlwind into heaven.

**12** And Elisha saw it and he cried, My father, my father! The chariot of Israel and its horsemen! And he saw him no more. And he took hold of his own clothes and tore them in two pieces.

**13** He took up also the mantle of Elijah that fell from him and went back and stood by the bank of the Jordan.

**14** And he took the mantle that fell from Elijah and struck the waters and said, Where is the Lord, the God of Elijah? And when he had struck the waters, they parted this way and that, and Elisha went over.

To emphasize his point the Angel directed me to the scripture above and proceeded to explain the principle again in this light. He showed me that the Prophet Elijah was an evolutionist, a Pioneer in Prophetic Manifestation which qualified him for spiritual fatherhood, however no one in his day received him as such until Elisha came on the scene. He pointed out that when Elisha's eyes were opened enough to see when Elijah was taken from him, the he cried out My Father, My Father. Elisha knew the dimension that Elijah was in at that moment. If you realize that on taking up the mantle of Elijah and returning to the river, he asked for the Lord God of Elijah before the struck the waters. He understood that it was Elijah's relationship with the Lord that he was now walking in and not his own.

## POINT: ANCESTRAL BLESSING

It is clear that the Lord is going to fulfil his promises in Isaac's life, not for his sake, but for Abraham's sake. We have to understand the principle that God blesses us through lineage and through divine connections.

We have to know who our present leaders' spiritual fathers are. We have to know the lives and anointings that they honor and respect, so we have an idea of the spiritual lineage in which they walk. They are blessings, anointings and favor that God wants to transfer to us because of spiritual heritage.

If you were to ask most of the great names in gospel ministry today about their spiritual heritage, I am certain they would make mention of another great man or woman of God that instructed them in the way of the Lord. Dr. Richard Roberts would tell you of his father Dr. Oral Roberts, Dr. Creflo Dollar would tell you of Kenneth Copeland, who would tell you of Dr. Oral Roberts. Dr. R.W. Shambach would tell you of Rev. A. A. Alleyne. Pastor Rod Parsley would tell you of Dr. Lester Sumrall, who if he was alive today would tell you of Howard Carter, who in turn would tell you of Smith Wrigglesworth. Apostle Frederick Price and Apostle Leroy Thompson would tell you of Dr. Kenneth Hagin. Pastor Benny Hinn would tell you Kathrine Koulman, and the list goes on.

In my own life I am a third generation minister. My Grandfather, the late Rev. Joseph Sobers, was a District Overseer in the

New Testament Church of God here in Barbados, and my father, Elder Edwin C. Scantlebury, became a minister in the same denominations in which I began the early days of my ministry. It was not until 2002, while ministering in the island of Anguilla that the Lord spoke to me about the direction that He was taking me in ministry. While sharing the word, the voice of the Lord came to me and said, "I'm about to give you a tithe of the ministry that I will cause you to eventually walk in." Instantly a very heavy presence came upon me and my knees bent and I started walking strangely.

I doubt that those who were there had any clue about what was happening to me. There was a young lady attending the service who was injured in a vehicular accident and she was wearing a collar around her neck. The Lord said to me, "I want you to stop preaching and go take that collar off her neck." I obeyed and the young lady was instantly healed. That anointing stayed on me for the next four hours into the early hours of the morning.

Then the Lord spoke to me again and said "When you return to Barbados, I want you to write a letter to Dr. Oral Roberts requesting an opportunity to see him; I will speak to him when he receives the letter and when you're going to him, take USD$1,000.00 with you." I received a call from the late Ruth Rooks, who at that time was Dr. Robert's secretary.

She told me that Dr. Roberts had instructed her to get in touch with me to set up the time for our meeting. In 2004

I travelled to California in the USA to meet with this great man of God, one of the Generals of Faith, and I had my seed of USD$1,000.00. I went to his home, where I met his wife Evelyn. As we sat I shared with him my experience and the instruction I received, and that I was there to hear what the Lord wanted to say to me through him. He leaned over and said "Son, the Lord spoke to me when I received your letter, but just last night he revealed to me what I should say to you today."

After sharing the word of the Lord, he then prophesied to and prayed with me. Then, amazingly, he asked me to pray for him, and I did (praise God). Within minutes of this happening his son Dr. Richard called and I had the chance to speak to him for the first time. I knew then that my spiritual heritage had a divine change.

I feel in my spirit that you may be due for a connection to or a change in spiritual heritage that will cause new and uncommon blessing, anointing, and favor to begin to come on your life. Go ahead and ask God to make that connection known to you.

CHAPTER 4

# LOOSE YOUR FEAR

**Gen 26:7**

**7** And the men of the place asked him about his wife, and he said, She is my sister; for he was afraid to say, She is my wife – [thinking], Lest the men of the place should kill me for Rebekah, because she is attractive and is beautiful to look upon.

In this aspect of receiving from the Angel, he began to emphasize the importance of living a fear free lifestyle and properly investigating any element or event so as to be adequately position to make informed decisions and to act in line with the divine.

He began to reveal that fear is triggered by mind-sets that are rooted in the consciousness of tragedy, failure and death. Fear works with internal triggers.

The men of Gerar simply asked Isaac a question about his wife Rebecca because she was a beautiful woman.

This simple question triggered Isaac's inner thinking and produced so much fear within him that he actually lied about his relationship with Rebecca. He said "she is my sister."

The Angel said to me that it's important to notice that Isaac thought the men would kill him because of her beauty.

Rebecca's beauty was an issue to Isaac in Gerar, just like the church's beauty today in glory, wealth and power is an issue to the world system and satanic forces.

The Angel said that many use this event with Isaac to teach on the subject of generational curses, but this is far from that. This is actually the result of the knowledge of the world systems having a negative impact on the psychology of the child of God and the Church.

## ABRAHAM'S EXPERIENCE

### Gen 12:10-16

**10** Now there was a famine in the land, and Abram went down into Egypt to live temporarily, for the famine in the land was oppressive (intense and grievous).

**11** And when he was about to enter into Egypt, he said to Sarai his wife, I know that you are beautiful to behold.

**12** So when the Egyptians see you, they will say, this is his wife; and they will kill me, but they will let you live.

**13** Say, I beg of you, that you are my sister, so that it may go well with me for your sake and my life will be spared because of you.

**14** And when Abram came into Egypt, the Egyptians saw that the woman was very beautiful.

**15** The princes of Pharaoh also saw her and commended her to Pharaoh, and she was taken into Pharaoh's house [harem].

**16** And he treated Abram well for her sake; he acquired sheep, oxen, he- donkeys, menservants, maidservants, she donkeys, and camels.

**17** But the Lord scourged Pharaoh and his household with serious plagues because of Sarai, Abram's wife.

**18** And Pharaoh called Abram and said, what is this that you have done to me? Why did you not tell me that she was your wife?

**19** Why did you say, she is my sister, so that I took her to be my wife? Now then, here is your wife; take her and get away [from here]!

**20** And Pharaoh commanded his men concerning him, and they brought him on his way with his wife and all that he had.

This chapter starts out with God speaking to the then Abram, asking him to leave his father's house and promising to bless him and make his name great, and using him to bless all nations. As Abram obeyed God and departed Ur of the Chaldeans, he took along Sarai and his nephew Lot. A severe famine engulfed the land and Abram went down to Egypt to dwell until the famine was over. Abram, knowing that the Kings of the earth had a habit of wanting the most beautiful women as their wives or objects of pleasure, and knowing that Sarai was a beautiful woman, planned with her to say that she was his sister, so that they would spare his life.

As soon as the Princes of Egypt saw her and asked Abram about her, he said "she is my sister," so the Princes said to themselves that a woman with such beauty must be the Pharaoh's wife, and they took her into the palace. In vs. 16, Pharaoh actually paid Abram for Sarai, and he accepted the payment. However, God intervened and plagued the household of Pharaoh for Sarai's sake. The entire royal family in Egypt became ill. This spelt trouble for the nation of Egypt.

The Pharaoh soon realized what the problem was, and he reasoned that the plague only started after he brought Sarai into his palace. He recognized that Abram had lied to him about Sarai. In his anger the Pharaoh restored Sarai to Abram and sent them out of Egypt. Abram was now very wealthy when he left. It would surprise you to know that Abram was not finished with his plan. Another account can be found in Genesis Chapter 20:

**Gen 20:1-10**

**1** NOW ABRAHAM journeyed from there toward the n South country (the Negeb) and dwelt between Kadesh and Shur; and he lived temporarily in Gerar.

**2** And Abraham said of Sarah his wife, She is my sister. And Abimelech king of Gerar sent and took Sarah [into his harem].

**3** But God came to Abimelech in a dream by night and said, Behold, you are a dead man because of the woman whom you have taken [as your own], for she is a man's wife.

**4** But Abimelech had not come near her, so he said, Lord, will you slay a people who are just and innocent?

**5** Did not the man tell me, She is my sister? And she herself said, He is my brother. In integrity of heart and innocency of hands I have done this.

**6** Then God said to him in the dream, Yes, I know you did this in the integrity of your heart, for it was I Who kept you back and spared you from sinning against Me; therefore I did not give you occasion to touch her.

**7** So now restore to the man his wife, for he is a prophet, and he will pray for you and you will live. But if you do not restore her [to him], know that you shall surely die, you and all who are yours.

**8** So Abimelech rose early in the morning and called all his servants and told them all these things; and the men were exceedingly filled with reverence and fear.

**9** Then Abimelech called Abraham and said to him, What have you done to us? And how have I offended you that you have brought on me and my kingdom a great sin? You have done to me what ought not to be done [to anyone].

**10** And Abimelech said to Abraham, What did you see [in us] that [justified] you in doing such a thing as this?

**11** And Abraham said, Because I thought, Surely there is no reverence or fear of God at all in this place, and they will slay me because of my wife.

**12** But truly, she is my sister; she is the daughter of my father but not of my mother; and she became my wife.

**13** When God caused me to wander from my father's house, I said to her, This kindness you can show me: at every place we stop, say of me, He is my brother.

**14** Then Abimelech took sheep and oxen and male and female slaves and gave them to Abraham and restored to him Sarah his wife.

**15** And Abimelech said, Behold, my land is before you; dwell wherever it pleases you.

**16** And to Sarah he said, Behold, I have given this brother of yours a thousand pieces of silver; see, it is to compensate you [for all that has occurred] and to vindicate your honor before all who are with you; before all men you are cleared and compensated.

**17** So Abraham prayed to God, and God healed Abimelech and his wife and his female slaves, and they bore children,

**18** For the Lord had closed fast the wombs of all in Abimelech's household because of Sarah, Abraham's wife.

This time Abraham (formerly Abram) went down to Gerar and pulled the same plan on King Abimelech. He said to the men of the city that Sarah was his sister and not his wife. Sarah was taken away into the palace, and for the second time Abraham was without his wife because of his scheme. Again God intervened by visiting King Abimelech and ordering him to give Sarah back to Abraham.

This time Sarah was supernaturally protected by God while she was in the palace; God also stopped Abimelech from having any offspring. God closed the wombs of the King's wife and all the female slaves. Once more the royal family was affected because of Abraham and Sarah.

When questioned by King Abimelech about his deceptive action, Abraham revealed his thought process fully. He **said "I thought that there is no fear of God in Gerar."** He explained that Sarah was really his half-sister, and when God instructed him to leave Ur of the Chaldeans, he planned this scheme with her. Interestingly enough,

God told King Abimelech that Abraham was a Prophet, and that he would pray for him. God used Abraham to bring healing to the King's household. The Angel explained to me that the problem wasn't the Government or culture of Gerar, but how Abraham allowed the information to affect his thought process. It was proven that there was a residue of the fear of God there.

He said that it becomes difficult to truly trust God when worldly information affects the mind negatively. It takes the mind away from totally believing, trusting and walking in the power of the word of God with boldness.

Even though God had made promise to Abraham, Abraham still continued his way of thinking where the world around him was concerned.

The Angel said "Lynroy, do you see that these events aren't related due to a generational curse of any kind. It is the result of allowing information about the world around us to be mentally processed in a negative way that makes the child of God act in fear'.

He, like the church today, saw the world as ungodly. As long as we do this, we will never see the open doors for the blessing opportunity.

It is at this point that the Angel said something to me that troubled me greatly. He said, "Notice that in all the accounts, the actions of both Abraham and Isaac brought about serious effects on the governmental systems. Abimelech even told Isaac that he would've destroyed his whole nation of one of the men had taken Rebecca. It's because of the thinking and action of the Church that is many time responsible for the crises we see in nations of the world."

He said "Due to the teaching of Isaac sowing in famine many ministers began conjuring up schemes and financial events to exact money from the Body of Christ and wealthy business people. He said that a level of extortion has been manifested in the Body of Christ, and this has been combined with the financial corruption in the world system to create a constant reoccurrences of worldwide financial crises. The season for correction is here."

CHAPTER 5

# LET YOUR IGNORANCE BE CONFRONTED

**Gen 26:8-10**

When he had been there a long time, Abimelech king of the Philistines looked out of a window and saw Isaac caressing Rebekah his wife.

**9** And Abimelech called Isaac and said, See here, she is certainly your wife! How did you [dare] say to me, She is my sister? And Isaac said to him, Because I thought, Lest I die on account of her.

**10** And Abimelech said, What is this you have done to us? One of the men might easily have lain with your wife, and you would have brought guilt and sin upon us.

As we reached this critical aspect of the visitation, the Angel began to open up my understanding in a greater measure. He explained that the revelations of God require a certain level of understanding that will allow me to by-pass the thresholds that creates ignorance and misunderstanding.

He went on to explain that Isaac stayed in Gerar as a guest of the King Abimelech, and therefore was treated with dignity. Isaac was there for a long time and he was not in any financial difficulties, neither was he struggling or under duress, and he certainly was not in any famine as originally taught.

Notice that for the length of time he was in Gerar, Isaac did not sow any seed or engage in any known form of business. The reason for this is that he had improperly positioned himself in Gerar due to his scheming.

He didn't even realize that even though he told them that Rabecca was his sister, they didn't take her from him. They allow him and her to live together under his brother and sister act. The Angel said that this should've opened Isacc's mind that something had changed in Gerar.

One day the King looked out of his window and saw Isaac caressing Rebecca, and he instantly knew that Rebecca was Isaac's wife.

Seeing Isaac in this position certainly made Abimelech very angry.he asked Isaac two serious questions... How did you [dare] say to me, She is my sister? What is this you have done to us? He expressed to Isaac that his actions would have caused national chaos if one of the men had lain with Rebecca.

Isaac's response was this...Because I thought, lest I die on account of her.

Isaac revealed that his action was the result of an old way of thinking about the governance and culture of Gerar. This level of thinking positioned him and his wife improperly in that land while they were there.

The Angel opened my eyes to the reality that King Abimelech had to clearly explain to Isaac that the nation was no longer in that form of thinking after the experience with his father Abraham. The King continued to explain to Isaac that if one of the men of the Gerar would have lain with Rebecca under the assumption of her being his sister, that he would've affected the whole nation negatively.

As the Angel continued with his explanation, he said to me, "Lynroy you must understand that in the nations of the world, a church operating improperly can be directly responsible for the ills that plague them."

At this point I began to see that the church must come out of our improper thought processes, change our paradigm and embrace new spiritual, financial, personal, business and political ways of thinking in an ever- changing world.

As I studied this carefully, the Angel said "I want to show you what Abimelech really saw from a deeper spiritual perspective when he looked through his window and saw

Isaac caressing Rebecca." He saw Christ and his Church in agreement to deceive him and his nation. This is a traditional, present day view of the Church and ministers. Many people believe that Jesus and the whole concept of Christianity is nothing more than an attempt to brainwash the people of the world. If King Abimelech was not a man of resolve he could have had Isaac arrested or even killed for his folly."

Thankfully, Abimelech knew what had happened previously with Abraham. He knew about the prophetic anointing that was on Abraham and the great miracle that was performed through him. The King knew that Isaac was the son of a powerful man.

## Point: KNOW YOUR COVENANT

The Angel said to me that Isaac's behavior in Gerar was a matter of ignorance. Before he was born, Abraham and King Abimelech had made a covenant not to deal falsely with each other or with their descendants after them. Isaac was totally unaware of this.

Abimelech asked Abraham to swear to him by his God. He did not even include his own gods because he saw the power of the God of Abraham. Unlike Isaac, in this age we cannot afford as children of the Lord to walk in the earth blissfully ignorant of the covenant of God which we have by virtue of being in Christ and in his blood. We have to be in the knowledge of our covenant rights as believers in the earth, and learn how to enforce those rights.

## Gen 21:22-23

**22** At that time Abimelech and Phicol the commander of his army said to Abraham, God is with you in everything you do.

**23** So now, swear to me here by God that you will not deal falsely with me or with my son or with my posterity; but as I have dealt with you kindly, you will do the same with me and with the land in which you have sojourned.

Abraham and Abimelech, it demanded that their offspring be honestly and kindly dealt with in the earth. This covenant is so powerful that the awesomeness of its strength and might is only clearly seen when you interpret the names of the two men involved. Abraham means: Father of a multitude, while Abimelech means: Father of the King. So here we see the Father of Nations and the Father of the King making a covenant.

In Gerar, King Abimelech knew what he had to do with Isaac. He knew the covenant that he and Abraham made and he wasn't going to break it.

God had established a covenant for Isaac to eventually walk in beforehand. A covenant that would guarantee his safety and preservation in the midst of a harsh world system and order. Even though Isaac was in fear, in actuality he really had nothing to worry about.

It's vitally important for us to know our covenant in this season as children of God.

CHAPTER 6

# THE ORDER OF PROTECTION

**Gen 26:11**

**11** Then Abimelech charged all his people, He who touches this man or his wife shall surely be put to death.

In dealing with this situation of discovering Isaac's deception, the Angel began to reveal the power of King Abimelech's response. He showed me that he responded in a manner that was totally unexpected by Isaac, his government and his people.

To their utter amazement, He made a national declaration and placed an order of protection on Isaac and his family. Any Philistine touching Isaac or his wife would be put to death. This declaration would have come as a shock to the people Gerar. Why would the King make such a command? An entire nation was commanded not to touch one man and his family.

Obviously there must be something special about Isaac to place such a national seal of security on him. What the people of Gerar didn't know was that the King was enforcing the covenant that he had originally made with Abraham years ago. This order of protection, or diplomatic immunity, instantly lifted the fear of dying that was lingering and revolving in Isaac's mind. He was now free from the mental and operational restrictions he had placed on himself as a result of his deceit. With this single declaration, Isaac was instantly recognized as a person of high importance in Gerar.

This gave him freedom of movement and leverage. It allowed him the opportunity to begin creating strategy, brainstorming, and investigating areas in Gerar that could be potential income earners. Another way of explaining this is to say that he was given the keys to the city. Even though Isaac may not have been liked by some in Gerar, everyone had to respect him. Isaac had the equivalent of a national security clearance status on his life. When you have this level of national security status, you're free to operate differently. You do not function as though you are confined or restricted. You have flexibility of action and freedom of movement.

At this point Isaac was free to meet with key persons in Gerar, he was free to create new partnership, share his ideas and vision, and make deals with those in the upper echelon of society in the nation.

The angel went on to explain that what King Abimelech did for Isaac allowed him to maximize his potential and also expose the nation to a man who had in him the blessing of God.

He said to me, "Do you see it Lynroy, it takes a high level of divine protection on your life that will allow you the freedom you need to move into new and greater levels of experience, existence, success and prosperity in the earth realm. So just as King Abimelech offered such protection to Isaac in his day, so now the Lord wants to give his people his highest level of protection in their day, so they can exceed and excel in the areas where he has assigned for them."

I began to see that Isaac's new found freedom, and everything he undertook in Gerar was the result of having that Order of Protection over his life, and he used it to its fullest.

In continuing to emphasize this point, the Angel said, "Many in the Body of Christ and in the world live without the knowledge of and the need for higher levels of divine protection over their lives, ministries and businesses, at this is the reason that failure enters and aborts what God had intended to do. This higher level protection is the key for the God kind of success that's missing from the body of Christ and believers today. For example, if you look at the account of the Prophet Malachai in his third chapter, he says this...

**Mal 3:10-12**

**10** Bring all the tithes (the whole tenth of your income) into the storehouse, that there may be food in My house, and prove Me now by it, says the Lord of hosts, if I will not open the windows of heaven for you and pour you out a blessing, that there shall not be room enough to receive it. [Mal 2:2.]

**11** And I will rebuke the devourer [insects and plagues] for your sakes and he shall not destroy the fruits of your ground, neither shall your vine drop its fruit before the time in the field, says the Lord of hosts.

**12** And all nations shall call you happy and blessed, for you shall be a land of delight, says the Lord of hosts. AMP

If you focus on the eleventh verse, you will see the higher level protection from the Lord of Host. The word rebuke there speaks of pushing back with violent force, and this is what we haven't been able to do for many who are unaware of this vitally important principle."

As I continued to listen to the Angel, he went on to reveal how the tithe is a connection exchange point for the higher levels of outpouring and divine protection. He said that as Angels and guardians of the earth and humanity, they watch many Christians establish ministries and businesses without seeking to have them spiritually protected. He said that this can be done by having connection with a spiritual leader who possesses the ability from the Holy Spirit to cause the superior dimension to function at their command. They must be endowed with special spiritual ability to restrict and remove satanic forces.

He said that on a higher dimension of understanding this revelation, you must again revisit the meaning of the name Abimelech. It means Father of the King. When Abimelech (Father of the King) gave Isaac the order of protection, it was the Father of the King (the satanic ruler) over Gerar that was really being stopped. So Abimelech not only stopped his people from touching Isaac, but he also stopped the satanic ruler over Gerar from touching him.

So both heaven and earth were suspended and only Isaac was mobile. This is the new dimension of the body of Christ in the earth.

This was the beginning of the process that leads to Isaac achieving the hundredfold manifestation. So your level of divine protection is directly related to your success and prosperity in the earth.

In the Body of Christ an understanding must come that there is a divine link in having life, ministry and business protection through spiritual power and spiritual connection.

## THE PERSONAL WORD

The Angel then began to speak to me personally about the visitation in greater detail. He said, "Lynroy know that this is the reason we have come to you in this time and season, to make you know and understand the new things that is about to happen in the earth. We have chosen you to grant you the gift and power of divine high level protection to release over the nations and people of God, for the season of supernatural blessing, grace and favour is here, to lift them into a new dimension of success and prosperity in every area of their lives. We will now cause miracles and works of power that will increase them and prosper them in the midst of season of economic instability and distress. We will cause a new day of spiritual awakening to come to the nations of the earth, and much money will begin to move again, but this time in the right way, and you must release this high level protection upon the people as they give and sow. They will rejoice and glorify the Father, and walk in the power of Jesus Christ. We are with you."

As I received this impartation my entire being rejoiced at being selected to be a part of the Kingdom of God's rebuilding process in the earth and in the body of Christ. I rejoiced at knowing that a greater day of glory is manifesting in the earth, and that the Kingdom of God is bringing a higher level of protection to its people in all nations of the earth.

CHAPTER 7

# SOW WITH KNOWLEDGE

**Gen 26:12**

**12** Then Isaac sowed seed in that land and received in the same year a hundred times as much as he had planted, and the Lord favored him with blessings.

This verse conveys the title of this book, and clearly reveals the power behind Isaac's decision to engage in heavy agricultural exploits in Gerar. It was now very clear to me that Isaac did not sow seed in the time of famine, but rather after he was given the Order of Protection by King Abimelech.

Hence: Then Isaac Sowed.

The Angel at this point began to increase his presence and power in the visitation, and this was revealed as necessary to create the capacity to expand my soul to receive greater consciousness on this subject.

He began to share with me that in his new found freedom in Gerar, Isaac's entrepreneurial skills took over and no one in Gerar could touch him in anything he attempted to do. He was in a position where he was unchallenged. This lead Isaac to embark of a massive agro-industry project, he did it simply because he was a farmer; he had that mind-set and training from his father Abraham. He was just doing what he was accustomed to doing in his country.

For Isaac to instantly begin the process of sowing seed in Gerar, means that access to land of his choice was given to him by the King. This is the element of great favour.

## THE HUNDREDFOLD

The Angel said to me, "I must now open your understanding to the truth of the process of the working and manifestation of the hundredfold which Isaac received in the year he began to sow. Firstly, all the parameters were right for this to happen within the time frame that it did. It was a combination of several elements working in harmony to create what isaac's hundredfold."

The Angel went on to list the parameters for the Hundredfold manifestation as:

- The Right Place
- Divine Favor and Blessing
- The High Level Protection

- The Sowing
- The Performance of the Abrahamic Oath

## Gen 26:3

**3** Dwell temporarily in this land and I will be with you and will favor you with blessings; for to you and to your descendants I will give all these lands, and I will perform the oath which I swore to Abraham your father. AMP

He continued to reveal that with the addition of the decree by King Abimelech, the system was now complete and all that was left was for Isaac to begin to sow. Once Isaac sows his seed, the next element was for the Lord to apply the oath of Abraham to the equation over a period of time during that same year.

He said the hundredfold is really dependant on the power and conditions exerted on the seed that was sown by Isaac by the divine realm. This divine power and conditions can determine to time frame of the hundredfold multiplication. In Isaac's case, it happened in the same year that he sowed.

This speed of return of the hundredfold shows that the power and conditions influenced the seed that was sown by Isaac to yield at maximum capacity. It was a hundred times as much as he had sown. This meant that we multiplied the seed; we touched Isaac's seed while it was in the earth.

Now beyond this, I want you to see a truth about Isaac that was important to this manifestation. Notice that the verse says that *he received in the same year.* We knew that Isaac was capable of receiving what we were doing on his behalf.

Likewise for this to happen as we planned in this season, more individuals in the Body of Christ must elevate themselves to becoming better receivers of the levels of success that we will be releasing. The hundredfold manifestation is a divine gift of power focused on an individual and the works of their hands.

You must understand that when we speak of a person being a receiver. We are referring to an individual who through a fuller comprehension of the promise of God can be spiritually reprogramed consciously to fully allow us to carry out the assignment in perfection in spite of the current conditions.

Let me show you how Jesus explains it...

### Mark 10:29-30

**29** Jesus said, Truly I tell you, there is no one who has given up *and* left house or brothers or sisters or mother or father or children or lands for My sake and for the Gospel's

**30** *Who will not receive* a hundred times as much now in this time – houses and brothers and sisters and mothers and children and lands, with persecutions – and in the age to come, eternal life. AMP

**Matt 13:23**

**23** As for what was sown on good soil, this is *he who hears the Word and grasps and comprehends it;* he indeed bears fruit and yields in one case a hundred times as much as was sown, in another sixty times as much, and in another thirty. AMP

"Do you see it", the Angel asked me. Do you see that the hundredfold is the result of the individual being a receiver and one who comprehends the word.

It wasn't until Isaac received the Order of Protection from King Abimelech that he began to fully comprehend the promise of the Lord which he spoke to him. Once he reached this level of spiritual consciousness, we were able to give him the hundredfold manifestation.

## THE HUNDREDFOLD PROBLEM

The problem of not experiencing the hundredfold in the body of Christ as the Angel of the Lord expressed was due to the preaching and teaching that Isaac sowed in the time of famine and miraculously received the hundredfold.

Once individuals accepted this as a conscious belief, many of them were then improperly conditioned to begin the process of moving and sowing finances in an effort to achieve this wonderful manifestation. However we were unable to cause it to be done, because we cannot break divine law.

This hurtful mind set of Isaac sowing in famine caused to many individuals to end up waiting on the manifestation of the hundredfold after they had sown financially, only to see nothing happen. This has led many to no longer have faith in this word or manifestation, and this is an element that we are attempting to correct by giving you this revelation, grace and commissioning. We need them to believe fully in our ability to make this a reality in their lives.

The Angel further revealed that as believers, we must understand that all of God's laws for dominion in this earth realm must be served, which means that the individual must be fully conscious of what they are doing when they're doing it. He then showed me two verses of scripture.

### Rom 7:25

**25** O thank God! [He will!] Through Jesus Christ (the Anointed One) our Lord! So then indeed I, of myself with the mind *and* heart, serve the Law of God, but with the flesh the law of sin. AMP

### Heb 11:17-19

**17** By faith Abraham, when he was put to the test [while the testing of his faith was still in progress], shad already brought Isaac for an offering; he who had gladly received *and* welcomed [God's] promises was ready to sacrifice his only son

**18** Of whom it was said, Through Isaac shall your descendants be reckoned

**19** For he reasoned that God was able to raise [him] up even from among the dead. Indeed in the sense that Isaac was figuratively dead [potentially sacrificed], he did [actually] receive him back from the dead. AMP

What these verses reveals is the truth that God's laws are served with the mind and heart, and secondly the Abraham was very much in control of what he was doing when he was asked to sacrifice Isaac. It said that he reckoned or he consciously figured out the level of the power God would have to manifest if he obeyed.

Abraham was convinced that God would have to actually resurrect Isaac from the dead, because He (God) had originally told him that in Isaac his seed would be called. So Abraham learned how to serve God with is mind and heart.

It is then imperative that more individuals achieve this level of maturity and development in this season and be ready for this next move of heaven in the earth in the aspect of the hundredfold.

## Point: EXPONENTIAL INCREASE POWER

Now on a higher level of knowledge, the Angel said that he must take me on a certain threshold of thought. This dealt primarily with the power that produces the hundredfold manifestation.

The Angel asked me "do you understand the power it took to make Isaac's seed reproduce on such a level of return, and the fact that we had to maintain this power in his life and business for over a year?

At this point I began to realize why my consciousness needed to be expanded, because this level of spiritual sight into the word wasn't in my mind.

He went on explaining that the angelic gathering over Gerar was mighty, and we knew that we had limited time to manifest this hundredfold for Isaac. We had to do this quickly, hence he words...In the same Year... because it was the Lord's desire to put Isaac above his enemies in wealth and in status, and to create a dimension of dominion for him. It is dominion that is missing for the body of Christ today, and the wheels are now set in motion to reclaim it.

## PERSONAL WORD

On saying this, the Angel spoke to me and said. "As you begin to teach this and implant this revelation into the body of Christ, and individuals begin to fully understand the principles and power of the hundredfold, and respond properly in their sowing, we will again have the opportunity to release the same power we gave to Isaac in Gerar. We will directly work with individuals, families, leaders, business persons who are touch to reach out to the Lord to claim this wonderful gift that's rightfully theirs in this season and those which are to come. We will cause a rapid rate in the allotted time frame for the manifestation of the hundredfold. God is going to cause things with us to change rapidly in an exponential way. We are going to be amazed at the speed of the turnaround in the Body of Christ worldwide. There is going to be an unbelievable chain of divine events that are going to manifest in your life. You and I are going to have surpassing victories. We are now ready to release and manifest the hundredfold in the earth on the scale never seen before, so prepare yourself and rejoice."

## Point: THE BLESSING PRINCIPLE

### Gen 26:12

...and the Lord favored him with blessings.

Again I felt when the Angel began to increase his presence in my room, and instantly in knew what it was for. I knew that my consciousness was being expanded to receive something greater, and I was very excited to receive it.

The Angel started to speak to me in a way that my comprehension was just able to decode. He specifically zeroed in on the element of the Blessing and explained that more understanding of the function of the blessing was needed to fully grasp what was done for Isaac in Gerar.

He said that the critical element of the Lord favouring Isaac with blessings is seen completely different by Angel as in comparison to human beings. As it concerns Angels, we see blessing as words of certain kind of power being spoken into an individual's life and time that organizes and orchestrates their lives in accordance with divine will and purpose.

He said, "I will now take you into a greater consciousness of the blessing of the Lord that will help you with this book and in the affairs of your life and ministry from here onwards." The Hebrew word for Bless is the word Barak, and when written in English, it looks like this: krb. So it is the Hebrew letters beth, resh, kaph. Beth meaning House, Tent, Covering, Ancestry, Resh meaning Head, and Kaph meaning Palm of the hand. Now when you put these together Lynroy, you get this... The house of the head and palms of the hands.

He went on explaining that you get the power and inheritance based on the house you're from, and if you study the bible carefully you will see that the Father usually selects person who are descendants of a particular house.

Understand that the blessing is the combination of the commission, gift of power, inheritance and prophetic future of a house spoken by the Father over and into the life of a patriarch to establish continuity and fulfilment of the divine will and purpose in the earth.

Now to help you fully understand this, I have to take you to the declaration made by Isaac's father Abraham when he spoke the King of Sodom...

**Gen 14:22-23**

**22** But Abram said to the king of Sodom, I have lifted up my hand and sworn to the Lord, God Most High, the Possessor and Maker of heaven and earth,

**23** That I would not take a thread or a shoelace or anything that is yours, lest you should say, I have made Abram rich. AMP

"Do you see where Abraham's hands and head were?" Are you beginning to see it clearly? The Angel said.

Besides this, David understood this principle clearly when he said...

**Ps 23:6**

**6** Surely or only goodness, mercy, and unfailing love shall follow me all the days of my life, and through the length of my days the house of the Lord [and His presence] shall be my dwelling place. AMP

Going further, he shared Jesus's revelation of being in the right house...

**Matt 19:29**

**29** And anyone and everyone who has left houses or brothers or sisters or father or mother or children or lands for My name's sake will receive many [even a hundred] times more and will inherit eternal life. AMP

Jesus said if the individual has left house, meaning what is covering them spiritually, and then the family connection, and switch to my covering, then the Hundredfold is a guarantee.

My eyes were now opened spiritually to this visitation and to the reality of the fruit it was to produce. I began to realise that Isaac was of the right house for such an amazing manifestation of the hundredfold to take place in his life.

## THE SHIFT OF BLESSING

The Angel began a systemic pulsation of his presence, and I could hear a particular frequency in my ear, as he started to show me a hidden truth about the blessing.

He showed me that as Angels they saw when the blessing in Isaac's life was shifted from Abraham to the Lord. We saw when Isaac was taken into the House of the Lord, and at that point we had to rapidly expand his borders and scope of success and prosperity.

He made me understand that the Blessing of Abraham is one House, but the Blessing of the Lord is another house, and that a shift of blessing took place in Gerar.

The Angel explained that there was a difference between to two Blessings. The Blessing of Abraham was rooted in Salvation, but the Blessing of the Lord is rooted in Dominion.

He said that this is the reason why in salvation, Jesus Christ brought over the blessing of Abraham to the Gentiles...

**Gal 3:13-14**

**13** Christ purchased our freedom [redeeming us] from the curse (doom) of the Law [and its condemnation] by [Himself] becoming a curse for us, for it is written [in the Scriptures], Cursed is everyone who hangs on a tree (is crucified); [Deut 21:23.]

**14** To the end that through [their receiving] Christ Jesus, the blessing [promised] to Abraham might come upon the Gentiles, so that we through faith might [all] receive [the realization of] the promise of the [Holy] Spirit. AMP

It was time for Isaac to have dominion. In addition, the blessing of the Lord carries a greater speed of return, respect and honour. At this point the Angel emphasised this verse of scripture that took on its full light when I looked at it...

**Prov 10:22**

**22** The blessing of the Lord – it makes [truly] rich, and He adds no sorrow with it [neither does toiling increase it]. AMP

"You see Lynroy, it is the blessing of the Lord that makes rich, and this must be understood as the key to walking in success in this realm for every believer."

Finally as it regards the blessing, the angel again showed me what he said is the original idea in the mind of the divine...

**Gen 4:4**

**4** And Abel brought of the firstborn of his flock and of the fat portions. And the Lord had respect and regard for Abel and for his offering, AMP

He said that this meant that Abel was at this moment received into the house of the Lord, and his head and hands were covered. The Lord respected and regarded for Abel and his gift. This elevated Abel into a superior place with the Lord.

# JACOB SAW US

## Gen 28:10-19

**10** And Jacob left Beersheba and went toward Haran.

**11** And he came to a certain place and stayed there overnight,
because the sun was set. Taking one of the stones of the
place, he put it under his head and lay down there to sleep.

**12** And he dreamed that there was a ladder set up on the
earth, and the top of it reached to heaven; and the angels
of God were ascending and descending on it!

**13** And behold, the Lord stood over and beside him and said, I
am the Lord, the God of Abraham your father [forefather] and
the God of Isaac; I will give to you and to your descendants
the land on which you are lying.

**14** And your offspring shall be as [countless as] the dust or
sand of the ground, and you shall spread abroad to the west
and the east and the north and the south; and by you and
your Offspring shall all the families of the earth be blessed
and bless themselves

**15** And behold, I am with you and will keep (watch over you
with care, take notice of) you wherever you may go, and I will
bring you back to this land; for I will not leave you until I have
done all of which I have told you.

**16** And Jacob awoke from his sleep and he said, Surely the Lord is in this place and I did not know it.

**17** He was afraid and said, How to be feared and reverenced is this place! This is none other than the house of God, and this is the gateway to heaven!

**18** And Jacob rose early in the morning and took the stone he had put under his head, and he set it up for a pillar (a monument to the vision in his dream), and he poured oil on its top [in dedication].

**19** And he named that place Bethel [the house of God]; but the name of that city was Luz at first. AMP

In proving his point and the blessing and what it truly was, he outlined to me that the Lord sought to continue the system with Jacob, by actually showing him how we were structured over his father's life. The Lord showed Jacob the ladder that we move on as we enter and exit the life of the one with whom we are instructed to function on behalf of. Jacob was shown our ascent and descent and he called that place the house of God.

He then showed me that Jesus Chist would later come and revealed that he was under the same house of God system...

## John 1:51

**51** Then He said to him, I assure you, most solemnly I tell you all, you shall see heaven opened, and the angels of God ascending and descending upon the Son of Man! AMP

Jesus knew and was working the blessing system all his days on the earth, and this was the key to his lavish success. Just as we help Isaac and Jacob, we help Jesus in his day and time.

Now as I pondered on this level of consciousness of these scriptures, the Angel began to explain to me that once they saw the blessings began to increase on Isaac, we knew exactly how to respond. We made people give him whatever he needed and we made them cooperated with him and limited any resistance that he would otherwise have received in Gerar,

As I listened intently to the Angel, I heard the greater voice saying, "The return of the hundredfold is here."

This kind of return was unbelievable to the eyes and minds of the Philistines, and they knew that there was something unusual about Isaac. He had something on his life that they didn't have; he had a connection to a superior power that surpassed the power of their deities and it was working for him day and night.

The day is here again for us to walk in the blessing of the Lord, and the people around us are going to recognize that there is something unusual operating in our lives. It time to be in the house of the Lord and claim our right to the hundredfold manifestation in every area of our lives.

Through the blessing, God is going to deliver the body of Christ from financial lack and bondage, and the world will watch in amazement as we are released form every restriction the world and satanic forces have afflicted us with.

CHAPTER 8

# BECOME INFLUENTIAL

**Gen 26:13-14**

**13** And the man became great and gained more and more until he became very wealthy and distinguished;

**14** He owned flocks, herds, and a great supply of servants, and the Philistines envied him.

As we approached this aspect of the visitation, the Angel said to me that there was a need for a dimension of deliverance that must be performed on me. He explained that I must be delivered from the fear of becoming too powerful and too wealthy, and also from the fear of what people will say when the hundredfold begins to manifests.

To be honest, I had absolutely no idea that I was living with this kind of fear in my life, but as I was shown by the Angel, most believers don't know the levels of fear that's blocking them form amazing experience in this realm.

I suddenly felt a level of courage entered my consciousness, and I knew at that moment that I was delivered.

In moving on to the next element of the revelation, the Angel said that Isaac's rapid increase and success was a phenomenon in Gerar. It was like everything he did was doomed to be prosperous.

Notice the statement, the man became great, and gained more and more, and had a great supply of servants. This is proof that he wasn't in this condition previously. Great is defined as 'unusual or considerable in degree, power, intensity, amount or dimension'. He became wealthy and distinguished in Gerar. The word 'distinguish' means to mark off as different. Through his God-given success, Isaac rose to a place of high influence and prominence in Gerar.

Isaac alone was changing the socio-economic climate in Gerar. He created an immense level of employment until he had a great number of servants.

## GREATNESS IS A GIFT FROM GOD

Now the Angel began to show me specific scriptures to reveal the truth that greatness is actually a gift from God. It is something that we can make happen to anyone who truly follows God's way and have been brought into the house of God.

## Gen 12:2

**2** And I will make of you a great nation, and I will bless you [with abundant increase of favors] and **make your name famous and distinguished**, and you will be a blessing [dispensing good to others]. AMP

## 1 Chron 29:12

**12** Both riches and honor come from You, and You reign over all. In Your hands are power and might; in **Your hands it is to make great and to give strength to all**. AMP

## Luke 1:31-32

**31** And listen! You will become pregnant and will give birth to a Son, and you shall call His name Jesus.

**32 He will be great (eminent)** and will be called the Son of the Most High; and the Lord God will give to Him the throne of His forefather David, AMP

God granted the gift of greatness to his chosen in the earth, and while others thought that it was a matter of luck or chance, it was the result of a gift from the Father that they couldn't see in action.

This gift of greatness caused Isaac to be the focal point of every arena in the land, especially in the political and business realms. The impact that Isaac's presence was having in Gerar was so immense that it affected the very spiritual. cultural, social, economic and political landscapes of the nation.

With a tone of joy in his voice, the Angel declared that this is the level God is taking the body of Christ into in this season. A season of the hundredfold is here changing everything rapidly and giving us genuine prosperity, success, greatness and influence that's needed for the people of God to have dominion in the earth and in their respective careers, countries and regions.

## Point: BE AN OWNER

The Angel began to point out a very important life result of the hundredfold in Isaac's life, and explained it to be what was said at the beginning of verse14 in the word: HE OWNED.

Isaac owned his possessions outright; he was not a debtor to any financial institution, government or person. Everything was his, no loan payments, no rental agreements, no letter of credit, he own it all free and clear.

Now understand that we will be assisting the body of Christ in owning things in this season, and this is more than a debt free anointing. This is to relieve the body of Christ from to reversal of the law of wealth that has been imposed on them by the satanic realm acting through the world system.

When I asked the Angel to explain more of this reversal of the law of wealth, he said to me that both lending and borrowing are parts of the divine law of wealth, but borrowing isn't to be used by use by the body of Christ for wealth creation initially as a practice. You are to LEND and NOT BORROW.

**Prov 22:7**

**7** The rich rule over the poor, and the borrower is servant to the lender. AMP

Once you fall into the state of being a borrower, you instantly become a servant.

When we own things, our state of being a borrower comes to an end and the hundredfold manifestation will be the point of change for the body of Christ to be set free from servitude dimension in this season.

Isaac's increase in his asset base and become financially free, removed him from the elements of the reversal of the law of wealth and the sleepless nights, stress and worry due to our financial situations will cease and become a thing of the past in our lives. We are going to walk in this anointing from the Lord; we are going to finally sound the 'all clear' from monthly payments, mortgages, car loans, credit cards and such like. We are going to be anointed for ownership. He is going to lift us up out of financial servanthood into a place of divine ownership manifestation.

We will no longer be controlled by this nemesis called debt that destroys our finances and takes our future from us. We will see the Lord work supernaturally with us, lifting us up out of financial servanthood into a manifestation of Divine Ownership. We are going to see many in the Body of Christ becoming owners of vast amounts of possessions; this will cause a supernatural ability and willingness to give to the work of the Body of Christ worldwide. The outflow from this anointing will be a blessing to the people and the nations of the world. Let's release our faith to the Lord for an ownership anointing now.

## Point: BECOMING MULTIFACETED

Another point that the Angel showed me relates to the flock and herd manifestation. Isaac developed multiple business streams and with this generated much wealth.

What he said was that believers must be capable of establishing many businesses and connecting with multiple influential persons.

The Angel said that flocks represent that which is moved within the local vicinity, but herds represent that which can be moved beyond the local borders. On a greater level of consciousness, he shared that flocks and herds represent divine ideas of multiplication and strength.

He went on to recall the case later with Jacob when he was at his uncle Laban, and how they showed him the higher idea to multiply the flock.

## Gen 31:10-12

**10** And I had a dream at the time the flock conceived. I looked up and saw that the rams which mated with the she-goats were streaked, speckled, and spotted.

**11** And the Angel of God said to me in the dream, Jacob. And I said, Here am I.

**12** And He said, Look up and see, all the rams which mate with the flock are streaked, speckled, and mottled; for I have seen all that Laban does to you. AMP

We showed Jacob how to think beyond the local sphere;, and by giving him this higher idea, he was able to enter into rapid wealth creation like his father Isaac.

So too in this time we will show individuals in the body of Christ certain higher dimensional idea, that will lift them out of a life od confinement into a life of blessing and freedom. The hundredfold will usher this in and many will receive.

With the supernatural increase that Isaac received, one of the notable effects was the abundance of servants that he acquired. The Angel spoke to me about this in a way that changed my way of thinking. He said: "Isaac's success significantly lowered the unemployment level in Gerar." I believe that as we obey the Lord through this revelation, the divine increase will cause us to lower the unemployment level in the Body of Christ and in the specific nation from which we function.

## Point: GOD HAS A REASON FOR OUR PROSPERITY

Isaac rapidly became one of the wealthiest men in Gerar. He now had servants from Gerar working in his businesses and in his house. He now had the opportunity to influence them with his teaching and knowledge of his God. The servants would've seen that Isaac wasn't worshipping their gods nor was following their customs, but yet he was excelling in everything he did. He had in one year changed the entire landscape of thought and operation in Gerar.

Isaac was able to create employment on multiple levels that enriched families and the nation of Gerar. He had flocks and herds and a great supply of servants.

In expanding my consciousness of the divine purpose for being wealthy, the Angel shared three things with me:

1. Having a seat and voice at the table of decision
2. Enjoying Life
3. Establishing God's Covenants

Understand that God has a reason for our prosperity, especially financial prosperity. When the blessing, favor, wisdom and power of God are working in our lives like in Isaac's, the prosperity that it brings creates influence in the earth. People begin to pay attention to you when you are successful and wealthy.

Understand that today our governmental decisions are greatly influenced by the wealthy in the earth. Entire nations are being led astray by wealthy individuals in the realms of politics, business, entertainment, education, pharmaceuticals, technology and media who have little or no sound moral, ethical or spiritual foundation, and who are connected to the satanic realm.

When we understand that God wants to cause us to prosper so that we can have a voice in these realms, then and only then we will begin to realize the power of Godly prosperity in the earth.

It is all God's plan for members of the Body of Christ to have dominion in the earth and not stand aside complaining about what the devil is doing and hoping for Jesus to return and rapture us away. They are great purposes that are yet to be fulfilled and much work to be done in returning the earth to the glory of the body of Christ.

Deuteronomy 8:18 says But you shall [earnestly] remember the Lord your God, for it is He Who gives you power to get wealth, that He may establish His covenant which He swore to your fathers, as it is this day. There is work to be done; there are lives to be saved and nations to be changed by the power of the Kingdom of God.

CHAPTER 9

# THE SECRET OATH OF ABRAHAM

**Gen 26:3**

and I will perform the oath which I swore to Abraham your father. AMP

I was specifically instructed to place this revelation at this point in the book by the Angel. For you who have made it to this point in your reading, something is about to happen to you.

The Angel said to me that he must show me the secret to the entire hundredfold manifestation in Gerar, how powerful and enjoyable it was for them to work on Isaac's behalf.

He told me the real secret was what the Lord told Isaac in Genesis 26:3, where he spoke about performing the oath of Abraham.

This oath of Abraham as the angel explained is complex to the untrained mind to grasp, but for those with a higher developed consciousness, it will become clear to them how they may claim it and walk in it on a daily basis.

Now and oath is defined as this...

a solemn promise, often invoking a divine witness, regarding one's future action or behavior.

Every oath requires a witness, but a witness that is greater than the person receiving the promise.

In Genesis Chapter 22, the Lord asked Abraham to sacrifice his son Isaac as a burnt offering. Abraham in faith obeyed and because of his obedience the Lord swore an oath to him and made some extraordinary promises to him.

However in the case of oath of Abraham, the one making the promises to him and the one swearing is the same.

### Gen 22:15-18

**15** The Angel of the Lord called to Abraham from heaven a second time

**16** And said, I have sworn by Myself, says the Lord, that since you have done this and have not withheld [from Me] or begrudged [giving Me] your son, your only son,

**17** In blessing I will bless you and in multiplying I will multiply your descendants like the stars of the heavens and like the sand on the seashore. And your Seed (Heir) will possess the gate of His enemies,

**18** And in your Seed [Christ] shall all the nations of the earth be blessed and [by Him] bless themselves, because you have heard and obeyed My voice. AMP

## Heb 6:13-14

**13** For when God made [His] promise to Abraham, He swore by Himself, since He had no one greater by whom to swear,

**14** Saying, Blessing I certainly will bless you and multiplying I will multiply you. AMP

When the Apostle Paul wrote about this he added this...

## Heb 6:16

**16** Men indeed swear by a greater [than themselves], and with them in all disputes the oath taken for confirmation is final [ending strife]. AMP

So seeing that there was no one greater with whom to swear by in his oath with Abraham, the Lord swore by himself, making this a very powerful oath. In other words, The Lord has to do this or He would have to dethrone Himself upon failure to manifest it in Abraham's life.

## THE OATH

The Angel said that it is important to breakdown the elements of the oath of Abraham in order to get a detail assessment of it. He continued to show me the intricacy of it in this manner.

1. Blessing and Multiplication like the Stars and Sand
2. The Descendant possessing the gate of his enemy
3. The blessing of the world through his Descendant

He said to me, "Do you see the amazingly powerful life that was promised to Abraham and his descendant?"

1. Greatness
2. Dominion
3. World Transformation

He continue by saying that he need at this time to take me into the greater truth of the oath of Abraham that actual on the highest dimension speaks towards Jesus Christ and not Isaac.

When the Apostle Paul spoke to the church in Galatia about the oath of Abraham, he correctly revealed that the promises in the oath were made to only two persons, namely Abraham and his seed, actual referring to Christ and not Isaac.

**Gal 3:16**

**16** Now the promises (covenants, agreements) were decreed and made to Abraham and his Seed (his Offspring, his Heir). He [God] does not say, And to seeds (descendants, heirs), as if referring to many persons, but, And to your Seed (your Descendant, your Heir), obviously referring to one individual, Who is [none other than] Christ (the Messiah). AMP

So in reality then only Abraham and Christ have the right to claim the manifestation of this oath. If God promised Isaac that he was going to perform the oath of Abraham in his life, then Isaac is going to experience what God planned to do in Jesus's life.

Indeed Isaac had to have all three elements of the oath of Abraham manifested during his time in Gerar. He became great, he had dominion over his enemies and he transformed Gerar.

## THE POWER OF CHRIST

In understanding what the Apostle Paul revealed, that the oath of Abraham was promised to Christ, and that only the Christ had to right to claim its manifestation, we have to speed forward to the main event of the reception of the oath of Abraham in Christ's life.

The Angel said that we have to go to the account of the Apostle Matthew in order to truly see when Christ to the manifestation of the oath of Abraham on his life and ministry.

**Matt 16:16-20**

**16** Simon Peter replied, You are the Christ, the Son of the living God.

**17** Then Jesus answered him, Blessed (happy, fortunate, and to be envied) are you, Simon Bar-Jonah. For flesh and blood [men] have not revealed this to you, but My Father Who is in heaven.

**18** And I tell you, you are Peter [Greek, Petros – a large piece of rock], and on this rock [Greek, petra – a huge rock like Gibraltar] I will build My church, and the gates of Hades (the powers of the infernal region) shall not overpower it [or be strong to its detriment or hold out against it].

**19** I will give you the keys of the kingdom of heaven; and whatever you bind (declare to be improper and unlawful) on earth must be what is already bound in heaven; and whatever you loose (declare lawful) on earth must be what is already loosed in heaven. [Isa 22:22.]

**20** Then He sternly and strictly charged and warned the disciples to tell no one that He was Jesus the Christ. AMP

One of the most important aspects of Jesus's life was to get the revelation of the Father. He had to be revealed by the Father in order to claim the Oath of Abraham in is life and ministry.

Jesus repeatedly asked his disciples what people were saying about him and what they personally thought about him. However on this occasion while arriving at Ceasaria Phillipi, Jesus asked his disciples the question again, but this time something different happened.

When he asked his disciples about their conceptualization of him, Peter said "You are the Christ the son of the Living God." At that point Jesus instantly blessed him and told him that it was the Father that had revealed who he truly was to him.

This is the truth of how it should happen according to the word, for Luke says...

**Luke 10:22**

**22** All things have been given over into My power by My Father; and no one knows Who the Son is except the Father, or Who the Father is except the Son and anyone to whom the Son may choose to reveal and make Him known. AMP

The Angel revealed to me that once the Father had revealed the Christ, he now had the full right to claim the oath of Abraham in is life and ministry.

He said that on paying closer inspection to the text in Matthew 16, Jesus instantly blessed Peter and changed his name; he said he will begin to build his church and the gates of Hades will not be able to prevail and finally he said that he will give them the keys of the Kingdom.

What Jesus did was that he activated the oath of Abraham to very moment that the Father revealed to Peter that he was the Christ. Notice that he strictly charged them not to tell people that he was the Christ. It's the Father's job to reveal the Christ, not man's.

In concluding this principle on the Christ, we have to again look at the key revelation given by the Apostle Paul concerning being in Christ. This is one of the greatest revelations given in the word of God.

The Angel revealed to me that the revelation of being in Christ means to exist in the original thought and idea of the Father in regards to who he created the Christ to be. There is a perfection an individual walks in when they truly understand the revelation of being in Christ Jesus.

**Gal 3:26-29**

**26** For in Christ Jesus you are all sons of God through faith.

**27** For as many [of you] as were baptized into Christ [into a spiritual union and communion with Christ, the Anointed One, the Messiah] have put on (clothed yourselves with) Christ.

**28** There is [now no distinction] neither Jew nor Greek, there is neither slave nor free, there is not male and female; for you are all one in Christ Jesus.

**29** And if you belong to Christ [are in Him Who is Abraham's Seed], <u>then you are Abraham's offspring and [spiritual] heirs according to promise</u>. AMP

Notice that the Apostle Paul clearly reveals that in Christ, in the original thought and idea of the Father regarding the Christ, the child of God are all sons. Secondly he says that through baptism believers have put on Christ like a garment. Thirdly he says, nationality, economic status, and gender are removed in Christ, and finally he says that if you belong to Christ you are Abraham's offspring and heirs according to the promise.

- IN CHRIST
- All Sons of God
- We wear Christ as a garment
- No Nationalities
- Economic Equality
- No Gender

Keep in mind that the oath of Abraham according to the revelation of the Apostle Paul was made to Abraham and his seed, which is Christ. So being in Christ, putting him on and belonging to him, guarantees that all believers upon realizing this truth can actually claim the oath of Abraham to manifest in their lives just as it happened with Isaac and with Jesus Christ.

He asked me, "Do you really see why you have been chosen to receive this revelation, and why it is important for it to be released to the body of Christ today? Too many believers aren't activating this oath of Abraham in their lives because they simply are unaware of it. We can help them change their lives and bring them into the hundredfold if they are will to obey."

As I pondered the words of the Angel, I couldn't resist the truth or power with which he spoke. I realized that I had not been using my place in Christ properly and that it wasn't God's fault for the lack of success and prosperity in my own life and ministry. The truth is therefore revealed that all believers can prosper.

I knew that my entire concept of this must change since I grew up in church hearing that God doesn't want everyone to prosper of have money. Today many even preach this or claim that there is no prosperity message.

However the Angel of the Lord has cleared this from my mind and heart, and I have fully accepted the hundredfold and the oath of Abraham as a reality in my life. I want to challenge you to do the same today.

CHAPTER 10

# SUCCESS CREATES ENEMIES

**Gen 26:14-15**

and the Philistines envied him.

**15** Now all the wells which his father's servants had dug in the days of Abraham his father, the Philistines had closed and filled with earth.

On reaching this aspect of the text, the Angel began to share with me a very eye opening element of habitual generational evil. This speaks mostly to the habits of the forces of evil that are implemented against the righteous to block pending prosperity, especially if the prosperity is lavish.

He revealed that the Philistines had an evil habit that started back in the days of Abraham and continued into Isaac's time. This evil habit was seizing wells of others or secretly filling wells in with soil. This was a something they would do on a regular basis if they consider that the individual was accumulating wealth too rapidly.

The Philistines began to envy the prosperity of Isaac so much that they tried to undermine him. Isaac wasn't as spiritually evolved as his father Abraham and this proved to be a partial problem. Isaac found out that his father had dug a number of well in Gerar that were his by right, but after Abraham died the Philistines filled all the wells in with stuff.

It was as though they were saying that since Abraham is dead, these wells no longer have an owner. It was as though they didn't expect Abraham's son to come that way in his life. This was a sinister attempt on the part of the Philistines to block the transferal of blessing and possessions to the rightful heir.

They no longer wanted Isaac in Gerar, for it became clear to them that his success and prosperity wasn't based on the wells of his father. They were totally blown away by seeing such massive crop yielding with all of the wells closed. Notice carefully that these were the wells that Abraham's servants dug so they belonged to Abraham free and clear. The Philistines were wrong for filling them in.

In filling those wells with stuff, the Philistines we trespassing and attempting to hide a vital portion of Isaac's already establish inheritance in Gerar.

**In the name of Jesus Christ I release Angels to you, to stop your enemies from filling in your wells, hiding vital information from you and blocking your right to be successful and prosperous.**

The body of Christ must understand that it is always the world plan to despise or block their success and prosperity. Jesus reminded us that this will be the case when he said...

### Mark 10:29-30

**29** Jesus said, Truly I tell you, there is no one who has given up and left house or brothers or sisters or mother or father or children or lands for My sake and for the Gospel's

**30** Who will not receive a hundred times as much now in this time – houses and brothers and sisters and mothers and children and lands, **with persecutions** – and in the age to come, eternal life. AMP

Jesus said that the hundredfold will come with persecution, but for those who can handle the persecution, a new age of eternal life will come.

## GENERATIONAL EVIL

In the days when Abraham was in Gerar, a situation occurred that as his wife's maid Hagar, had left the house with her son Ismael. As she journeyed she found dehydrated and her son on the verge of dying.

Supernaturally we appeared to her and opened her eyes, and showed her a well where she and her son could drink and be refreshed.

**Gen 21:19**

**19** Then God opened her eyes and she saw a well of water; and she went and filled the [empty] bottle with water and caused the youth to drink. AMP

On retuning to Abraham and Sarah, Hagar informed Abraham about the well that was shown to her, and he went in search of it. Abraham found the well and claimed it.

On learning of the same well the men of Gerar seized it from Abraham and sought to claim it as their own.

**Gen 21:25-26**

**25** When Abraham complained to and reasoned with Abimelech about a well of water [Abimelech's] servants had violently seized,

**26** Abimelech said, I know not who did this thing; you did not tell me, and I did not hear of it until today. AMP

## SEEK HELP EARLY

Abraham complained to King Abimelech about the actions of the men of Gerar, and the King told him that he wasn't aware of the seizure of the well, and that Abraham didn't inform him of it.

So it's clear to see here that if Abraham had spoken to the King when the seizure took place, the matter would've been resolved that very moment.

Many times as believers, we delay in speaking to the relevant individuals about our situations. We delay in getting the help we need in order to change, or to have a better chance of a speedy resolution to our situations in this life.

The Angel shared with me that even though the men of Gerar had possession of the well for a season; the Lord eventually created an opportunity for it to be returned into Abraham's hands free and clear.THIS was a supernaturally revealed well and Abraham needed to own it. Through owning this well, it instantly became Isaac's inheritance in Gerar.

## OWNING THE WELL

### Gen 21:28-31

**27** So Abraham took sheep and oxen and gave them to Abimelech, and the two men made a league or covenant.

**28** Abraham set apart seven ewe lambs of the flock,

**29** And Abimelech said to Abraham, What do these seven ewe lambs which you have set apart mean?

**30** He said, You are to accept these seven ewe lambs from me as a witness for me that I dug this well.

**31** Therefore that place was called Beersheba [well of the oath], because there both parties swore an oath.

The Angel revealed that Abraham knew the significance of this, and he knew that he needed to own it. What we see in the verses above is Abraham securing to ownership of the well by establishing an oath with King Abimelech in giving him seven ewe lambs.

Now this may not seem like anything spiritual to King Abimelech, but Abraham knew exactly what he was doing. The Angel pointed out that the seven ewe lambs represented the eyes of the seven dimensions of wisdom. Abraham told King Abimelech that the seven ewe (female) lambs are the ones that witness that he dug the well.

Abraham named the place Beersheba which means well of oath.

**Prov 15:3**

**3** The eyes of the Lord are in every place, keeping watch upon the evil and the good. AMP

## Point: NEGOTIATE WITH WISDOM

Abraham was able to move quickly and act wisely in order to secure the well. He also had the spiritual knowledge to use the seven ewe lambs as part of his deal with the King. The body of Christ today must begin to demonstrate a higher level of godly wisdom and skill in operating within the world as it relates to securing the right framework and paperwork in elements of acquisitions, sales, deals and overall negotiation procedures especially in legal matters.

Due to Abraham's oath with King Abimelech, Isaac had the right to the well at Beersheba, and no one could stop him from laying claim to it.

### Matt 11:19

Yet wisdom is justified and vindicated by what she does (her deeds) and by I her children. AMP

The Angel said that it is very important to have someone in our lives that can witness to what is rightfully ours. We have seen many live in the earth and never appropriate with is theirs by will or by ancestry. We have seen many live in poverty due to being cheated out land, houses, building, money and opportunities all due to not having the wisdom to create the right agreements or secure the necessary documentation to master the legal parameters that may arise.

The body of Christ must become the catalyst for change in the world in the area new technological advancements, improvements and innovations and fulfil our God-given mandate in the earth. As we start businesses, ministries, new projects, and create new inventions, it is going to be important that we understand the legal principles of copyrighting, title deeds, branding and incorporating if we are going to safeguard our products and ideas.

As we obey the Lord in this season of correction, there are going to be widespread, rapid results in the lives of God's children worldwide, and we have to expect that it will not go down well with those who are actively against the prosperity and success of the righteous.

CHAPTER 11

# HANDLE PERSECUTION

**Gen 26:16**

**16** And Abimelech said to Isaac, Go away from us, for you are much mightier than we are. AMP

Isaacs's prosperity and success took him to a dimension that he became so great that alone he was mightier than King Abimelech and his people, so in an effort to avert the pending altercation between Isaac and the men of Gerar he asked Isaac to leave.

Gerar actually became too small for Isaac's immense fortune and status. That level of ascension in wealth and status in the life of a child of God is testimony to the true blessing of God backed by his power, promises and oath.

Isaac staying in Gerar would certainly lead to dispute, and King Abimelech took action, knowing that if he didn't, he would most likely have to carry out his order to put persons to death for touching Isaac. On learning of the escalation in aggressive behaviour towards Isaac, King Abimelech knew that it would be better for Isaac to leave Gerar.

Remember that Gerar means dispute, combat and pilgrimage, and now Isaac was about to see the meaning of this place confront him openly.

The Angel instructed me to find the Greek word and meaning of persecution, and on doing so, this is what I found...

## PERSECUTE

Dioko

To put to flight, drive away, to pursue.

In applying the Greek meaning of the word to the sudden turn of events in Gerar, it is clear to see that Isaac came under heavy persecution.

### Gen 26:17

**17** So Isaac went away from there and pitched his tent in the Valley of Gerar, and dwelt there. AMP

In his response to the King's request, Isaac didn't complain or even sought to take any defensive action. He simply handled the situation by closing his businesses, packing up his good and family, and relocated to the valley areas of Gerar.

## SIGN OF THE FUTURE

The Angel continued to pour into my spirit insight and truth about the reality of the hundredfold and the oath of Abraham. He explained that since the oath was promised to Abraham and Christ, Isaac was the actual test subject and hence he was a type of Christ.

I reality what happened with Isaac must happen in the life of Jesus Christ for the fulfilment of the oath to be proven as authentic.

He said that he must take me to an account in Luke chapter 8.

### Luke 8:26-28

**26** Then they came to the country of the Gerasenes, which is opposite Galilee.

**27** Now when Jesus stepped out on land, there met Him a certain man out of the town who had [was possessed by] demons. For a long time he had worn no clothes, and he lived not in a house but in the tombs.

**28** And when he saw Jesus, he raised a deep (terrible) cry [from the depths of his throat] and fell down before Him [in terror] and shouted loudly, What have You [to do] with me, Jesus, Son of the Most High God? [What have we in common?] I beg You, do not torment me! AMP

Thousands of years later, Jesus Christ journeyed in to Gerar as the true recipient of the oath of Abraham. The moment that He stepped on the land, He was instantly met by a man that was possessed by demons for a long time, that he lived in the tombs, and brought fear to everyone.

This demon spirit was so afraid of Jesus's presence there that he begged Him not to torment him.

Jesus expelled the demons from the man and restored him to his right mind. However something shocking took place afterwards when the people came out after hearing what had occurred.

### Luke 8:35-37

**35** And [people] went out to see what had occurred, and they came to Jesus and found the man from whom the demons had gone out, sitting at the feet of Jesus, clothed and in his right (sound) mind; and they were seized with alarm and fear.

**36** And those [also] who had seen it told them how he who had been possessed with demons was restored [to health].

**37** <u>Then all the people of the country surrounding the Gerasenes' district asked [Jesus] to depart from them</u>, for they were possessed and suffering with dread and terror; so He entered a boat and returned [to the west side of the Sea of Galilee]. AMP

The people of Gerar thousands of year later, asked Jesus to do the very same thing they asked Isaac to do in his day. They asked him to leave.

The Angel then said to me that this was the very spirit that persecuted Isaac, because he changed the city of Gerar and now it did the same thing with Jesus in his day when he changed the city of Gerar by giving a great deliverance to this man who was possessed with demons and relieve them of the fear of his presence.

So what happened in Gerar with Isaac was a sign of what was to come in the future with Jesus Christ. Even then the people were still suffering from the effects of the presence of the demons that existed in Gerar for centuries.

It takes someone knowing and walking in the oath of Abraham to have power to torment these lingering demonic spirits that have plagued nations of the world for ages.

At this point in began to clearly see an element of the oath of Abraham that speaks to Possessing the Gate of our enemy. What Jesus did in Gerar with the possess man was a clear sign the he was the Christ, that where ever he went he would take control of all territories that were held captive by the enemy.

The time is here for the body of Christ to understand what is behind the persecution in nations, its actually demonic spirits that have been lurking and hiding in territories to block the progress of believers and the church from changing people and nations in accordance with the divine will and purpose of God. Christianity must rise to a greater consciousness in this season, if we are to fulfil the commission of the Kingdom.

In concluding this aspect of the revelation, the Angel spoke to me about what was said to the Prophet Daniel in chapter 12 of his writings.

**Dan 12:1**

**1** AND AT that time [of the end] Michael shall arise, the great [angelic] prince who defends and has charge of your [Daniel's] people. And there shall be a time of trouble, straitness, and distress such as never was since there was a nation till that time. But at that time your people shall be delivered, everyone whose name shall be found written in the Book [of God's plan for His own]. AMP

The Kingdom of God is sending the Angels to deliver the Body of Christ. Get ready for it.

CHAPTER 12

# RECONNECT TO THE SUPERNATURAL

**Gen 26:17-18**

**17** So Isaac went away from there and pitched his tent in the Valley of Gerar, and dwelt there.

**18** And Isaac dug again the wells of water which had been dug in the days of Abraham his father, for the Philistines had stopped them after the death of Abraham; and he gave them the names by which his father had called them.

In exposing me to a greater reality of this revelation, the Angel said that Isaac, even though the King asked him to leave Gerar, Isaac didn't receive instruction from the Lord to do so, for the Lord had told him to dwell in the land. Isaac moved from the city limits to the valley area of Gerar. While there, he embarked on a massive plan to reopen the wells of his father Abraham, and gave them their names back.

This tells us that Isaac was aware of the wells that his father owned in Gerar, and also he knew them by their names which meant that he also knew the spiritual significance of each well.

Isaac knew that his father Abraham was a master of finding wells supernaturally, and that based on the location a name was given to the well that revealed an aspect of God's nature, and he lived by those revelations.

Abraham passed on this very special secret to his son Isaac, and after his partial exit of Gerar, he began to use it.

After Abraham's death the Philistines eventually realized Abraham's secret. They realized that Abraham was a well digger and that he believed that his God alone owned the earth, and by filling these wells up, they believed that they were stopping the power of Abraham's God in the earth. They would never again have to deal with such a blessed man in the earth. Unfortunately, Isaac came along and shattered their plan.

When Isaac began to reopen the wells of his father, it was a picture of him reconnecting to spiritual dimension and to the principles that governed Abraham's life; it was a sign that he was making supernatural revelation his guide for living again. It was a sign that he was going to walk in the ways of his father before the Lord.

## SECRET REVELATION

The Angel said that only Abraham and Isaac knew the names of these wells. This means that Abraham and Isaac lived with secret insight and wisdom that the Philistines didn't have.

Likewise today, in order for the body of Christ to operate above and beyond the world, they are secret that must be known by it.

This is what Jesus practised throughout his ministry by speaking to the people in parables. He did this for a particular reason which he eventually told to his disciples.

### Matt 13:10-11

**10** Then the disciples came to Him and said, Why do You speak to them in parables?

**11** And He replied to them, To you it has been given to know the secrets and mysteries of the kingdom of heaven, but to them it has not been given. AMP

Jesus explained to his disciples that the reason for parables is to create a method of speaking to the mass, but still hide the secret information for them. He said to the disciple they were given the opportunity to know the mysteries and secrets of the Kingdom, but the masses weren't given that opportunity.

This means that the disciples were chosen to live and operate in a higher level of knowledge and consciousness than the people around them.

On another occasion, Jesus spoke to his disciples about the parable of the sower. What was interesting about this is that on explaining the parable to his disciples, He told them that if they don't discern this particular parable, then it will not be possible for them to understand all other parables.

So in reality Jesus taught that all the parables are based on a single revelation.

### Mark 4:13-14

**13** And He said to them, Do you not discern and understand this parable? How then is it possible for you to discern and understand all the parables?

**14** The sower sows the Word. AMP

The body of Christ has a sacred responsibility to live in the earth realm by supernatural laws, revelations, mysteries and secrets of the Kingdom of God. The knowledge of these secrets lifts the body of Christ into new dimension of spiritual experiences that are difficult for the untrained unreeled minds of others to receive.

# A CRY OF WISDOM

## Prov 1:20-23

**20** Wisdom cries aloud in the street, she raises her voice in the markets;

**21** She cries at the head of the noisy intersections [in the chief gathering places]; at the entrance of the city gates she speaks:

**22** How long, O simple ones [open to evil], will you love being simple? And the scoffers delight in scoffing and [self-confident] fools hate knowledge?

**23** If you will turn (repent) and give heed to my reproof, behold, I [Wisdom] will pour out my spirit upon you, I will make my words known to you. AMP

In revealing his verse of scripture, the Angel announced that a new day of Godly wisdom has come. Wisdom has been seeking to get the attention of individuals in the streets, businesses places, governments and judiciary, because she's seen a huge problem in the earth. She's seen that people love being simple, full of self-confidence and haters of knowledge, and she wants to stop it urgently.

Wisdom says that if you will repent and listen to her instructions, she will pour out her spirit and will give her revelations.

In adding to this, the Apostle Paul in his message to the Ephesians said that he prays that God would grant them the spirit of wisdom and revelation in the Knowledge of God.

**Eph 1:17**

**17** [For I always pray to] the God of our Lord Jesus Christ, the Father of glory, that He may grant you a spirit of wisdom and revelation [of insight into mysteries and secrets] in the [deep and intimate] knowledge of Him, AMP

He clearly understood the importance of the body of Christ having the higher level wisdom and knowledge of God that the world didn't have. Notice what he further said to the Corinthians...

**1 Cor 2:6-7**

**6** Yet when we are among the full-grown (spiritually mature Christians who are ripe in understanding), we do impart a [higher] wisdom (the knowledge of the divine plan previously hidden); but it is indeed not a wisdom of this present age or of this world nor of the leaders and rulers of this age, who are being brought to nothing and are doomed to pass away.

**7** But rather what we are setting forth is a wisdom of God once hidden [from the human understanding] and now revealed to us by God — [that wisdom] which God devised and decreed before the ages for our glorification [to lift us into the glory of His presence]. AMP

The Angel said to me that this hidden wisdom is presently available and that it is vital for request for the wisdom, knowledge and creativity of God to be made by believers who are ready for a greater level of experience of the deeper things of God.

The body of Christ must not allow the world to overtake them in the acquisition of secret knowledge and mysteries. This will cause a shift in the balance of power in the earth, and governments will begin to believe that they can have absolute control of nations without involving the word or the Spirit of God in their decision making processes.

It is time like Isaac did to reopen the wells of divine revelation and draw the water out and refresh the people of God. They are there waiting for someone to be bold enough to do it.

### John 4:14

**14** But whoever takes a drink of the water that I will give him shall never, no never, be thirsty any more. But the water that I will give him shall become a spring of water welling up (flowing, bubbling) [continually] within him unto (into, for) eternal life. AMP

CHAPTER 13

# THE LORD WILL OPEN YOUR EYES

## Point: LIVE BY REVELATION

The Angel, at this point said that in order to receive the understand of the power that Abraham began to walked in, he said that he had to take me back to beginning of the manifestation of that they created for him.

He said that it all started with Abraham receiving the gift of spiritual sight from the Lord, this spiritual sight gave Abraham the ability to see what the average person couldn't see. This ability affected every element of Abraham's life and everyone around him. This also guaranteed that those connected with him would be assisted by us the Angelic host. We were commissioned to fix all of his problems, and the problems of those associated with him.

In the verse below gives an understanding of how the process of spiritual sight was activated in his life.

### Gen 13:14-15

**14** The Lord said to Abram after Lot had left him, Lift up now your eyes and look from the place where you are, northward and southward and eastward and westward;

**15** For all the land which you see I will give to you and to your posterity forever.AMP

### Gen 15:5

**5** And He brought him outside [his tent into the starlight] and said, Look now toward the heavens and count the stars – if you are able to number them. Then He said to him, So shall your descendants be. AMP

With this ability granted to him, things were set in motion for his life to follow a certain path that would lead to complete fulfilment of the divine will and purpose.

## FINDING WELLS

Abraham's wife Sarah had a an Egyptian maid named Hagar, whom after realizing that she was unable to give children to Abraham, asked him to take her maid as produce a child with her. This seemed like a reasonable plan, but after becoming pregnant, Sarah and Hagar began to have some issues and this lead to Hagar leaving Abraham and Sarah.

The Angel showed here that it was at this point that they intervened in the situation.

**Gen 16:7-10**

**7** But the Angel of the Lord found her by a spring of water in the wilderness on the road to Shur.

**8** And He said, Hagar, Sarai's maid, where did you come from, and where are you intending to go? And she said, I am running away from my mistress Sarai.

**9** The Angel of the Lord said to her, Go back to your mistress and [humbly] submit to her control.

**10** Also the Angel of the Lord said to her, I will multiply your descendants exceedingly, so that they shall not be numbered for multitude.

**11** And the Angel of the Lord continued, See now, you are with child and shall bear a son, and shall call his name Ishmael [God hears], because the Lord has heard and paid attention to your affliction.

**12** And he [Ishmael] will be as a e wild ass among men; his hand will be against every man and every man's hand against him, and he will live to the east and on the borders of all his kinsmen.

**13** So she called the name of the Lord Who spoke to her, You are a God of seeing, for she said, Have I [not] even here [in the wilderness] looked upon Him Who sees me [and lived]? Or have I here also seen [the future purposes or designs of] Him Who sees me?

**14** Therefore the well was called Beer-lahai-roi [A well to the Living One Who sees me]; it is between Kadesh and Bered.

He said we opened her eyes spiritually and showed her this well of water, and she named it Beerlahairoi meaning the Living One who sees me.

Notice it says that the well is between Kadesh which mean Holiness and Bered which means to Hail or Salute. So this well was strategically located. It speaks spiritually of an individual that's living in a secret place with God, where the eyes of God are constantly on the person.

## HAGAR'S EYES OPENED AGAIN

On another occasion, this time after the birth of Hagar's son Ismael, the Lord visited Sarah and caused her to give birth to a son whom the Abraham named Isaac. As Isaac and Ismael grew together, it happened that Sarah was watching to two boys play, but Ismael began to persecute Isaac, and this caused Sarah to become very angry.

With this anger, she went and asked her husband Abraham to send away both Hagar and her son Ismael. This didn't sit well with Abraham, but the Lord advised him to listen to his wife.

Abraham prepared provision and sent away Hagar and her son, and this is when another intervention was made.

**Gen 21:14-19**

**14** So Abraham rose early in the morning and took bread and a bottle of water and gave them to Hagar, putting them on her shoulders, and he sent her and the youth away. And she wandered on [aimlessly] and lost her way in the wilderness of Beersheba.

**15** When the water in the bottle was all gone, Hagar caused the youth to lie down under one of the shrubs.

**16** Then she went and sat down opposite him a good way off, about a bowshot, for she said, Let me not see the death of the lad. And as she sat down opposite him, he lifted up his voice and wept and she raised her voice and wept.

**17** And God heard the voice of the youth, and the angel of God called to Hagar out of heaven and said to her, What troubles you, Hagar? Fear not, for God has heard the voice of the youth where he is.

**18** Arise, raise up the youth and support him with your hand, for I intend to make him a great nation.

**19** Then God opened her eyes and she saw a well of water; and she went and filled the [empty] bottle with water and caused the youth to drink. AMP

The Angel said that on two separate occasions Hagar, Abraham's maid, came into the knowledge of wells supernaturally. The Lord opened her eyes and she was able to see wells that to normal person wouldn't have seen.

On learning of this manifestation with Hagar, Abraham learnt the principle of having the Lord open your eyes at a specific moment to see His supernatural provision.

In Genesis chapter 22, Abraham had learnt and mastered this belief of the open eye for supernatural provision, that the Lord tested him in asking him to sacrifice his only son Isaac. Abraham instantly obeyed, and while journeying to the place where he was to perform the sacrifice, Isaac who was now a grown young man asked him a question...

## Gen 22:7-8

**7** And Isaac said to Abraham, My father! And he said, Here I am, my son. [Isaac] said, See, here are the fire and the wood, but where is the lamb for the burnt sacrifice?

**8** Abraham said, My son, God Himself will provide a lamb for the burnt offering. So the two went on together. AMP

When Abraham was asked where was the lamb for the sacrifice, Abraham who was now very developed in his belief of the open eye for supernatural provision, replied to his son with a sure confession of the Lord's ability to open his eyes and show him His provision.

The Lord honoured Abrahams faith and belief, and provided him a ram that was caught by its horns in a bush on the very mountain he went to sacrifice Isaac.

**Gen 22:13**

**13** Then Abraham looked up and glanced around, and behold, behind him was a ram caught in a thicket by his horns. And Abraham went and took the ram and offered it up for a burnt offering and an ascending sacrifice instead of his son! AMP

Abraham passed on this secret for living to his son Isaac, and he understood exactly how his father wanted him to conduct his affairs before the Lord.

I want to ask you to pray about having the faith and belief of Abraham to walk with the Lord knowing that he will open our eyes to see His supernatural provision throughout your life.

**Gen 25:11**

**11** After the death of Abraham, God blessed his son Isaac, and Isaac dwelt at Beer-lahai-roi [A well to the Living One Who sees me]. AMP

Isaac learned the principle of living in the place of the revelation of the Lord---living in the place where God is the living one who sees.

In this time, as the Lord corrects us, he will open our eyes and cause us to see the supernatural realm and it will begin to work for us again. The Lord will show us things we have never seen before. We are going to live by the revelations of the Lord. He will be revealing to us now and in times to come. God is going to show us where things are in the earth that he has never shown anyone else.

They are reserved for us. Just like the Philistines, the world system has done its best to fill up the spiritual wells of the Body of Christ in the earth. The enemy's plan is to cause us to become natural and materialistic in our approach to life and living in this earth realm.

His ultimate desire is to stop us from believing God and His ways of doing things. This demonic plan has gone on for so long in the earth and the day of the Angels of the Lord opening our eyes is here again.

As I said earlier, as the Lord revealed, the Philistines filled in the wells in an attempt to stop the supernatural, to cut God off, and prevent the emerging of another blessed man being manifested in the earth. It is time to unclog the inner wells of the power of God in our lives, and allow the supernatural powers of God to spring forth from our lives.

Based on the promises that Abraham and Isaac received, it is plain to see that they were encouraged to trust God and believe in his power for results in the earth.

In biblical times wells represented life source, wealth, health, sustenance and power. The secret was this, when you dug a well and found water, you opened the earth and caused it to see and reflect heaven. A well dug without finding water was a form of blindness.

The concept is this, the water in the well functioned as a mirror to the heavens above. When you caused the earth to see and reflect the heavens, you became a blessed man. So Abraham and Isaac dug wells as their eyes were opened by the Lord wherever they went and ultimately became blessed men. They learnt the secret of looking into the Spirit realm and living by the revelations that they received of the Lord. We have to go back to living our lives by the revelations of the Lord today.

## Eph 1:17-18

**17** [For I always pray to] the God of our Lord Jesus Christ, the Father of glory, that He may grant you a spirit of wisdom and revelation [of insight into mysteries and secrets] in the [deep and intimate] knowledge of Him,

**18** By having the eyes of your heart flooded with light, so that you can know and understand the hope to which He has called you, and how rich is His glorious inheritance in the saints (His set-apart ones).

One revelation from the Lord can change your life forever. The Body of Christ in the earth is responsible for causing the earth to see and reflect the heavens. What we must understand in our present day is this same well- digging concept that is now to be done in the inner man. Jesus promises that the water he will give us will be a well of water springing up into everlasting life.

### John 4:14

**14** But whoever takes a drink of the water that I will give him shall never, no never, be thirsty any more. But the water that I will give him shall become a spring of water welling up (flowing, bubbling) [continually] within him unto (into, for) eternal life.

He also says this...

### John 7:38

**38** He who believes in Me [who cleaves to and trusts in and relies on Me] as the Scripture has said, From his innermost being shall flow [continuously] springs and rivers of living water. AMP

**2 Cor 12:1**

**1** TRUE, THERE is nothing to be gained by it, but [as I am obliged] to boast, I will go on to visions and revelations of the Lord. AMP

When we begin to cause the earth to see heaven through living by the revelation of the Word of God, and having our eyes opened, we will become the blessed of the earth. We have to move into a mature dimension of Christianity if the world will begin to see us in the right light today.

## CHAPTER 14

# IT'S TIME FOR MORE ROOM

As we approached this level of the visitation, I began to feel a greater vibration of the Angel's presence and also a change in my awareness as though I could feel what was about to come next.

He began to reveal to me that as Isaac settled in the valley of Gerar, he was living in the power of the open eye, the he instructed his servant to begin digging wells.

**Gen 26:19-21**

**19** Now Isaac's servants dug in the valley and found there a well of living [spring] water.

**20** And the herdsmen of Gerar quarreled with Isaac's herdsmen, saying, The water is ours. And he named the well Esek [contention] because they quarreled with him.

**21** Then [his servants] dug another well, and they quarreled over that also; so he named it Sitnah [enmity].

Isaac's servants dug a well and made an amazing discovery. They found a well of living spring water, ad this excited Isaac and his servants very much. However, their excitement was short-lived.

Little did they know that the herdsmen of Gerar were secretly watching as they dug the well, and showed up at the very moment Isaac's servants found the water to engaged Isaac's servants in a quarrel for the well.

The herdsmen of Gerar contented that THE WATER WAS THEIR, and based on that, Isaac had no right to it even after his servants had done all the work in digging the well.

Isaac then instructed his servants to give up the wells, but he did something that was out of character. He named one well Esek meaning 'contention' because of the situation that had occurred.

Again Isaac's servants were successful at location another well, and sure enough the herdsmen of Gerar were watching again, and came to fight for this well. This time they gave no reason for their aggressive behaviour, but as before Isaac gave up the well. This time he named the well Sitnah meaning 'enmity'.

The Angel said to me that Isaac even though he had the sight, he didn't name to wells at the moment of discovery, he named them after the altercation with the herdsmen of

Gerar. He did not attach the finding to a revelation of God as his father did or even as Hagar did.

This is the point where the enemy can creep in and create opportunity to steal what we have laboured in building of finding in accordance to God's will.

## OPENED EYES NEEDS A QUICK MOUTH

In explaining this point, the Angel revealed that throughout the scripture, when anyone received a revelation of God, they were quick to give the place the encapsulated to manifestation of the revelation.

### Gen 22:14

**14** So Abraham called the name of that place The Lord Will Provide. And it is said to this day; on the mount of the Lord it will be provided. AMP

### Ex 17:15

**15** And Moses built an altar and called the name of it, The Lord is my Banner; AMP

Understand the secret here, that the open eye needs a quick open mouth to name the revelation of the Lord. Isaac naming the wells after the altercation between himself and the herdsmen of Gerar, is a reversal of the secret that was used by his father.

The Angel then took me to a particular scripture to show me the link between the spiritual eye and the mouth. He told me that when to spiritual eyes is opened, the mouth speaks in line with it at all times.

**2 Kings 6:15-18**

**15** When the servant of the man of God rose early and went out, behold, an army with horses and chariots were around the city. Elisha's servant said to him, Alas, my master! What shall we do?

**16** [Elisha] answered, Fear not; for those with us are more than those with them.

**17** Then Elisha prayed, Lord, I pray You, open his eyes that he may see. And the Lord opened the young man's eyes, and he saw, and behold, the mountain was full of horses and chariots of fire round about Elisha. AMP

This is the scriptural account of the Syrian Army who came to take the Prophet Elisha, who was using his prophetic powers to assist the King of Israel during the time of war.

The Syrian King had sent his army to seize the Prophet who was living in a place called Dothan. The word Dothan means 'two wells or double feast'. Therefore the prophet was living in a very powerful place.

When the servant to the Prophet woke up on a certain day, he was shocked to see the Syrian army surrounding Dothan, and this literally scared him to death. On awakening the Prophet Elijah, the servant informed him of the impending attack, and asked what was to be done.

Now notice the response from Elisha even though the natural circumstance was horrible and life threatening. The Angel said that the difference between Elisha and his servant, was the fact that Elisha's spiritual eyes were opened, so his mouth was quick to reveal what he was seeing. The servant's eyes were closed spiritually so his mouth was quick to speak only what he saw in the natural.

Elisha said, "Fear not; for those with us are more than those with them." Elisha was seeing the more through his opened eye. He then prayed to the Lord and asked Him to open the young servant's eyes, and the Lord instantly opened his eye, and he was able to see what the Prophet Elisha was seeing.

The Angel with a tone of excitement in his voice asked me, "Guess what the young man saw? He said, He saw us encircling Elisha, ready to defend and give him victory over his enemies."

I was then instructed to say to you as you have reached this point in the book, that the Lord will open your eyes, and you will see what you've never seen before, so you can do what you've never done before, in Jesus Name.

# THE WELL OF ROOM

## Gen 26:22

**22** And he moved away from there and dug another well, and for that one they did not quarrel. He named it Rehoboth [room], saying, For now the Lord has made room for us, and we shall be fruitful in the land. AMP

In spite of the situation between him and the herdsmen of Gerar, it didn't deter Isaac from continuing his plan of digging well. He advanced the situation by moving from that area so as to avoid any further incidents. According to the scripture Isaac dug a well in his new location and found water, but this time there was no quarrel for this one and so he named it Rehoboth, meaning 'room'. He spoke prophetically saying that the Lord had made room for them and that fruitfulness would come to them in the land.

Notice that this time around, Isaac applied the revelation of the Lord to his naming the well. The Angel started sharing with me the aspect of Isaac combining the room with the fruitfulness. The word room there is the Hebrew word 'bayit' which can signify rooms and or wings of or an added on portion to a house.

Isaac saw through his spiritual eye that the Lord had actually created a room for him, which guaranteed him that he was going to be fruitful in the land. Once Isaac had enetered that room all of his problems ceased.

The Angel said to me that he must make me understand the word of Jesus Christ which he spoke to his disciple in John 14, verse 1 and 2.

## John 14:1-3

**1** DO NOT let your hearts be troubled (distressed, agitated). You believe in and adhere to and trust in and rely on God; believe in and adhere to and trust in and rely also on Me.

**2** In My Father's house there are many dwelling places (homes). If it were not so, I would have told you; for I am going away to prepare a place for you.

**3** And when (if) I go and make ready a place for you, I will come back again and will take you to Myself, that where I am you may be also. AMP

Again another powerful surge of vibration came from the Angel, and of course, as I began to realize, a revelation was about to come. The Angel then said, "Many believe that the words of Jesus Christ here are referring to some impending rapture, some end time event, but I assure you Lynroy, this isn't about that. This is an on-going manifestation as the Holy Father makes and creates Spiritual rooms in His Kingdom for the life changes He desires in the lives of His chosen in the earth. Once the Holy Father positions an individual in that Spiritual Room, they are now set to carry out His divine will."

He said, "Notice what Jesus said how he goes to prepare a place the disciples, and not for himself, for Jesus knew that his room was already there. He needed the disciple to have their own spiritual room so that it would be possible for them to be where he was so that the disciples could behold him in his state of glory with the father."

The Angel said that this is the same principle used by the Lord used with the prophet Elijah when he was sent to anoint Elisha.

**1 Kings 19:16**

**16** And anoint Jehu son of Nimshi to be king over Israel, and anoint Elisha son of Shaphat of Abel-meholah to be prophet in your place. AMP

As you can see, Elisha was to eventually move into Elijah's place or room. This isn't just a replacement statement it is statement declaring the new occupant of the spiritual dimension.

## PERSONAL WORD

The Angel said, "So now it is here again, say to the nations of the world that the Holy Spirit is making room for the body of Christ. Spiritual rooms are being offered and prepared by the Holy Father and Jesus Christ to change lives to do greater work in the kingdom of God. Say to them that the time has come to open their minds and heart to greater good news and reality of things never seen before. Say to them to forget the former things and prepare for new things, for the glory light has come, and it is already shining upon the body of Christ. The new day is here go in strength that your emeries cannot resist for the Lord is with you to cause the Hundredfold to quickly become the reality in the lives of many."

I couldn't help but to stop writing for a while and give God praise for what he was about to do in my life and for the body of Christ in this season and beyond.

CHAPTER 15

# THE GOD OF PLACE

**Gen 26:23-25**

**23** Now he went up from there to Beersheba.

**24** And the Lord appeared to him the same night and said, I am the God of Abraham your father. Fear not, for I am with you and will favor you with blessings and multiply your descendants for the sake of My servant Abraham.

**25** And [Isaac] built an altar there and called on the name of the Lord and pitched his tent there; and there Isaac's servants were digging a well. AMP

The Angel began to draw my attention to what he called the Law of the Divine Place. He explained to me that only certain manifestations from God will happen at particular places that have been designated by the divine as spiritual high places. Once an individual reaches this place in the physical or in the spiritual realm, there is an instant response to them from the Holy Father.

The Law of Divine Place is a spiritual check point where the chosen person or persons, are anointed, empowered and commissioned for divine assignment, and it is also a point of coding into the living life and revelation of God.

After living for a period of time in the valley of Gerar, Isaac made a decision to go back to Beersheba. Remember Beersheba means `the well of oath'; it is where Abraham had given the seven ewes lambs to King Abimelech as a seal of him owning the well.

This turn out to be an excellent decision by Isaac. It was as though this was what the Lord was waiting on him to do, for as we see in the text, that the Lord appeared to Isaac the very same night that he arrived in Beersheba and spoke to him saying...And the Lord appeared to him the same night and said, I am the God of Abraham your father.

The Lord never spoke to Isaac while he was in the valley of Gerar, but as soon as he returned to Beersheba, the Lord appeared to him the same night. What are the odds of this happening the same night that he reached Beersheba (well of the oath)?

Not only did the Lord appeared to Isaac, He also spoke to him and promised him His presence, favor with blessings and multiplication of offspring for Abraham's sake. Remember I mentioned earlier about the Law of Place? This is a perfect example of that. God is the God of Place.

The Angel said to me that this is a revelation that must not be missed. Isaac returning to Beersheba is a spiritual sign of him returning to the original program and pattern set by God for Abraham and his descendants.

There was a certain way this family was to live and operate in the earth, that was totally and distinctly different from all other families. Beersheba was like a spiritual reconnection with the pre-set initiation program of God that was generated in Abraham.

Notice the Lord appeared to him and said I am the God of Abraham. What this means it that the same divine structure of presence and power that was given to Abraham, was now fully transferred into Isaac's life.

This visitation demonstrated that God manifests Himself on higher levels on you reach the place. He will not speak until you're at the place where He has determined to show Himself strong.

After the visitation, Isaac built an altar and called on the name of the Lord and erected his tent there, and it became his dwelling place. It is important to see how Isaac built the altar there. The word altar in Hebrew is Mizbeach, meaning a raised place where a sacrifice is made.

## BUILD AN ALTAR

Isaac built the altar as a sign to God that he is will to offer him whatever he wanted from him. Notice that nothing was sacrificed, he just built the altar.

Likewise individual in the body of Christ must create altars, raised places for honouring God in prayer, meditation and studying of the word, especially in their homes, and be in readiness to give God whatever He may request of them.

The Angel said that as they begin to work with the body of Christ in this season, many will find their way back to the designated physical and spiritual places. It will be very important for individuals and leaders to be ready and willing to engage in setting up new altars in their homes and families, churches, ministries, in communities, businesses and in the governmental realm. Schedule time for intense prayer and calling on the name of the Lord for His divine intervention will be crucial. As new shifting begins to take place in the areas of calling, ministry birthing, business establishment, careers, actual address changing and spiritual dimensions, that will be revealed to the children of God, maximum success and prosperity in the earth realm through the hundredfold will be the result. It will be as though their lives are being governed by the power of a larger universe that unseen by others.

He said that there is much work they will be doing in this new season, which will require the body of Christ to be ready and open to the move of the Holy Spirit. All of the gifts of the Holy Spirit will be utilized as we expand and increase to children of God around the world. It will be a season of great grace and rejoicing as the works of the enemy are brought to nothing.

Finally, notice that Isaac's servants continued to dig wells at Bersheba 'the well of oath'. This is a spiritual revelation that Isaac was seeking for more than what his father had found there. This must be the desire of the body of Christ today, a desire to go beyond where their forefather in the scriptures have gone and done. There must be a plan to keep digging until more and greater insight, revelation and power are discovered, so that the body of Christ may rise to its rightful place and glory in the earth.

The Angel said to me that the words of the God King David embodies this very ideal.

**Ps 27:4**

**4** One thing have I asked of the Lord, that will I seek, inquire for, and [insistently] require: that I may dwell in the house of the Lord [in His presence] all the days of my life, to behold and gaze upon the beauty [the sweet attractiveness and the delightful loveliness] of the Lord and to meditate, consider, and inquire in His temple. AMP

David's desire for more was the driving force behind is evolution into becoming the man after the heart of God. He wasn't playing with God in what he wanted to receive from him.

He said that it is necessary for the body of Christ today to do more than the previous body of Christ. Without this happening, Jesus's words will have proven to be false.

**John 14:12**

**12** I assure you, most solemnly I tell you, if anyone steadfastly believes in Me, he will himself be able to do the things that I do; and he will do even greater things than these, because I go to the Father. AMP

## CHAPTER 16

# KNOW WHO YOU ARE

This chapter was pointed out to me by the Angel as a very important one, because it deals with the aspect of personal psychology and spiritual perception. The Angel explained that having the knowledge of who you are in the sight of God is very important to how an individual assesses and processes situations in their lives, and wither they will find the strehgth to recover quickly and move on in life or wallow in self-pity and anger for years.

As Isaac settled in Beersheba, he began to experience a new resurgence of supernatural increase, he had experienced an even greater flow of results in this location. However to his surpise, he received an unannounced visit from King Abimelech, one of his friends named Ahuzzah, and Phicol his army commander.

**Gen 26:26-27**

**26** Then Abimelech went to him from Gerar with Ahuzzah, one of his friends, and Phicol, his army's commander.

**27** And Isaac said to them, Why have you come to me, seeing that you hate me and have sent me away from you? AMP

What we see here is Isaac still carrying a level of anger and resentment against King Abimelech for sending him away from Gerar. According to the text Isaac was of the opinion that Abimenlech had hated him, and that that was to reason why he asked him to leave.

If you noticed the response of King Abimelech, Isaac's emotional state of mind about what had occurred was far from reality. King Abimelech said that he sent him away because they saw that the Lord was with him. The governmental system of Gerar had gotten the revelation that Isaac was being helped by the superior presence of the Lord, and based on that principle alone is what lead King Abimelech to ask Isaac to leave.

The Angel said that there was no hatred involved in sending Isaac away, it was based solely on the revelation they had of him. Think about the length of time that Isaac was incubating the wrong mentality where his leaving Gerar was concerned. Therefore it was Isaac who was creating the hostility in his own mind, and maintaining it in his life.

We have to watch how we behave because of past situations. Manifesting a bad attitude towards individuals, because of things that have happened in the past and possessing damaged emotional state of mind can seriously affect what God wants to happen in our lives now and in the future.

Isaac's reaction to the King's presence at his home was not the way one should greet royalty. This was still the King who had made the order of protection over his life that gave him the freedom to pursue his desires in Gerar.

Here is where the Angel introduced this verse of scripture...

### Eccl 10:20

**20** Curse not the king, no, not even in your thoughts, and curse not the rich in your bedchamber, for a bird of the air will carry the voice, and a winged creature will tell the matter. AMP

He outlined here that our mental thought processes and incorrect mental states can make us engaged in blocking results and prosperity from us without knowing that we are actually doing it every day of our lives.

Becoming very stern in his voice, the Angel said, "do you recall the word of the Lord to Abraham when he called him in Genesis Chapter 12:3?"

### Gen 12:3

**3** And I will bless those who bless you [who confer prosperity or happiness upon you] and curse him who curses or uses insolent language toward you; in you will all the families and kindred of the earth be blessed [and by you they will bless themselves]. AMP

This reveals that the individual that speak, think and act well towards Abraham will receive blessing from the Lord, and likewise the individual that speak a curse, thinks and acts improperly towards Abraham will be cursed by the Lord.

Isaac's reacted to the King's visit improperly simply because he didn't know who he was, or he forgot who he was. He forgot that his very name meant Isaac meant "God Laughs", and in addition to have King Abimelech and his friends visit him to reveal that they saw that the Lord was with, was an even greater manifestation.

## BEWARE OF SELF SABOTAGE

As I continued to listen to the Angel reveal more about knowing yourself, he said that Isaac, as the Laughter of God, was stopping God from laughing through his distorted thinking. The word laugh in the Greek is the word "Gelao", which means a loud outburst by viewing something funny.

**Ps 2:1-4**

**1** WHY DO the nations assemble with commotion [uproar and confusion of voices], and why do the people imagine (meditate upon and devise) an empty scheme?

**2** The kings of the earth take their places; the rulers take counsel together against the Lord and His Anointed One (the Messiah, the Christ). They say, [Acts 4:25-27.]

**3** Let us break Their bands [of restraint] asunder and cast Their cords [of control] from us.

**4** He Who sits in the heavens laughs; the Lord has them in derision [and in supreme contempt He mocks them]. AMP

You see here how the enemy's plots and plans becomes a form of comedy for the Lord. So he Laughs Out Loud (lol).

Isaac was sabotaging his own life through improper thought processes. When King Abimelech and his friends told him that they saw that the Lord was with him, it instantly caused Isaac to release himself from the wrong consciousness of the past. Their words to Isaac made him realize that he was the one at the top, and that they themselves as men of power, recognized that he was in another dimension to them.

As the Angel proceeded to reveal more on this aspect, he said that he must explain to me, why they are certain things that God wants individuals to do, that they will never attempt until they know who they are.

## GOD WILL REVEAL WHO YOU ARE MOSES

**Ex 4:16-17**

**16** He shall speak for you to the people, acting as a mouthpiece for you, and you shall be as God to him.

**17** And you shall take this rod in your hand with which you shall work the signs [that prove I sent you]. AMP

## GIDEON

### Judg 7:13-15

**13** When Gideon arrived, behold, a man was telling a dream to his comrade. And he said, Behold, I dreamed a dream, and behold, <u>a cake of barley bread</u> tumbled into the camp of Midian and came to the tent and struck it so that it fell, and turned it upside down so that the tent lay flat.

**14** And his comrade replied, This is nothing else but the sword of Gideon son of Joash, a man of Israel. Into his hand God has given Midian and all the host.

**15** When Gideon heard the telling of the dream and its interpretation, he worshiped and returned to the camp of Israel and said, Arise, for the Lord has given into your hand the host of Midian. AMP

## JESUS

### Matt 16:16-18

**16** Simon Peter replied, <u>You are the Christ, the Son of the living God.</u>

**17** Then Jesus answered him, Blessed (happy, fortunate, and to be envied) are you, Simon Bar-Jonah. For flesh and blood [men] have not revealed this to you, but My Father Who is in heaven.

**18** And I tell you, you are Peter [Greek, Petros – a large piece of rock], and on this rock [Greek, petra – a huge rock like Gibraltar] I will build My church, and the gates of Hades (the powers of the infernal region) shall not overpower it [or be strong to its detriment or hold out against it]. AMP

The Angel said, "Look and see that in each case, once God had revealed to the individual in question, who they were, they instant began to do what he wanted them to do."

He added that the work of helping individuals in the body of Christ to know who they really are in the sight of God, will be a great part of the hundredfold manifestation, because we will need persons to think, speak and walk a particular way in the earth as we assist in returning the dominion in the earth to the children of God.

## DON'T JUDGE INCORRECTLY

As the Angel continued to reveal the truth of Isaac's experience, it became clear to me that he didn't use any spiritual discernment regarding the situation he previously encountered in Gerar. As the Lord is preparing to move on our behalf, I want to ask you to make an important decision, and that is to forgive whoever has wronged you in the past. God is giving you a new beginning, so let nothing block the supernatural from manifesting in your life fully. When we look at King Abimelech's and his entourage's response to Isaac's accusation, we realize just how wrong Isaac was thinking about the whole matter.

### Gen 45:4-5

**4** And Joseph said to his brothers, Come near to me, I pray you. And they did so. And he said, I am Joseph your brother, whom you sold into Egypt!

**5** But now, do not be distressed and disheartened or vexed and angry with yourselves because you sold me here, for God sent me ahead of you to preserve life. AMP

### Luke 23:34

**34** And Jesus prayed, Father, forgive them, for they know not what they do. AMP

These verses reveal a key principle for individuals who will encounter certain situations in life, though containing and produced by emotions and jealousy, or probably the very works of the enemy. What one must do is to pray to receive the God outcome in every situation so that you can take the position of forgiveness.

This in turn will keep you spirit and soul uncontaminated so as to perfect the divine journey, this keeping divine power at its maximum capacity. Once the divine power and presence are maintained, every situation must change and be constantly altered to work out in the favour of the one selected by God to experience it.

The Angel said that for those individual reading this book whose lives has be the result of divine power and presence operation with them in the way that constantly placed them in a better condition to the desire and work of their enemies, that the need to release through the act of forgiveness those involve in the attempt to block your path forward.

## THE LORD IS WITH YOU

### Gen 26:28-29

**28** They said, We saw that the Lord was certainly with you; so we said, Let there be now an oath between us [carrying a curse with it to befall the one who breaks it], even between you and us, and let us make a covenant with you

**29** That you will do us no harm, inasmuch as we have not touched you and have done to you nothing but good and have sent you away in peace. You are now the blessed or favored of the Lord! AMP

Coming into this aspect of the visitation, the Angel this time poured it my spirit a certain kind of energy the prepared me to go into the understanding of what was about to be revealed.

He said that after Isaac realized that King Abimelech and his friends had visited him due to having a revelation of him and not due to any hatred of him that he thought it further shocked him to be exposed to the true purpose of their visit.

King Abimelech told Isaac that he and his friends recognized that there was a supreme being giving Isaac the kind of results he was receiving in his life, and that due to their revelation, they had come to make a covenant with him.

## THE FLIP

Isaac probably couldn't believe that what he was hearing. This time around Abimelech and his friends are asking Isaac to establish a covenant with them, but the promises of the covenant are based on Isaac not attacking them.

The Angel said, "I want you to see that King Abimelech literally begged Isaac to make the covenant, he said... and let us make a covenant with you."

As I wrote earlier, King Abimelech, in Genesis 21:31, made a covenant with Isaac's father Abraham, and then he came to make an even greater covenant with Isaac.

## Point: THE POWER OF HIGHER LEVEL COVENANTS

This is absolutely powerful, to see King Abimelech coming to make this covenant with Isaac and bringing his associates as witnesses to his oath with him. The Angel said that he needed me to get the meanings of all the names involved in establishing the covenant.

- Isaac: God Laughs
- Abimelech: father of the king
- Ahuzzah: possession; seizing; collecting
- Phichol (Army Commander): the mouth of all; or every tongue

When we look at the revelations of the names of these men we realize that this is a very powerful covenant. In addition, it came with an oath that whoever broke the covenant will be put to death.

This covenant puts Isaac in his rightful place before God and in the earth realm. The Laughter of God is about to make a covenant with the King of the Father, who possesses all by the mouth of every tongue.

The Angel at this time pointed out the principle he had told me about earlier, that whatever happens to Isaac must eventually happen to Jesus Christ.

To prove this principle, when the Apostle Paul wrote by the Holy Spirit the revelation of Jesus Christ, he puts it like this:

### Phil 2:9-11

**9** Therefore [because He stooped so low] God has highly exalted Him and has o freely bestowed on Him the name that is above every name, 10 That in (at) the name of Jesus every knee p should (must) bow, in heaven and on earth and under the earth, 11 And every tongue [q frankly and openly] confess and acknowledge that Jesus Christ is Lord, to the glory of God the Father.

Picture this in your mind that in Genesis Chapter 26, the dominating King of the day, acknowledge the Lordship that was with Isaac, and bowed before him, seeking his protection through Isaac as the blessed of the Lord.

### Gen 26:29

**29** That you will do us no harm, inasmuch as we have not touched you and have done to you nothing but good and have sent you away in peace. You are now the blessed or favored of the Lord!

They obviously knew that Isaac place in the life of the Lord that was with him placed him in a position that was far above King Abimelech and his entire nation and dominion. They knew that Isaac's Lord had the ability to dismantle their lives and nation simply by touching Isaac in the wrong way.

Isaac was experiencing the flip to the previous experience while in Gerar, he was now giving out the order of protection on King Abimelech and his nation.

The Angel began to emphasize the point that the Body of Christ is oblivious to the reality of the knowledge of the Lord being with it, and what could happen to nations of the world for touching it in the wrong way.

The world has never been in this position regarding the church today, but we are about to see it happen in our day. We are going to see the switch in the spiritual realm and also in the natural realm. Never has the world come to us, but they will come to us now. We will become in the earth THE BLESSED OF THE LORD.

We are going to be seen by the world a manifested extension of the Lordship of Jesus Christ. They are agreement to be made and ministry to be offered to nations that will bring them into a relationship with the Father and he Lord Jesus Christ, that will cause widespread prosperity and blessing.

The Angel said that we have to prepare ourselves as the Lord begins to cause his power to go to work in our lives. The whole world is about to see a different body of Christ rise up in the earth, and they will respond in a way we have never seen with our own eyes.

What the Angel said to me about this in greater detail is that although governments have made agreements with the

Church fathers of old, they have been reluctant to make agreement with the sons of the present day churches and ministries whom they view as money hungry and false.

The Angel spoke saying, "Now the Kingdom of the Father is raising up a new church, a Hundredfold Church, with a clearer view and understanding of what I am doing in the earth, and I will cause Governments, business men and women to come to them for the plans to transform nations. This power will be released as a new age has come for the Body of Christ. Lift your head and rejoice for I will respond to your prayers in this hour. Many continue to preach and teach about end times and the time of the antichrist. They preach about destruction and the mark of the beast. But I am saying now No, No, No, my people will rule and have dominion in the earth and every nation in the earth will see my people obeying me and they will see me blessing my people. My people will no longer live like second class citizens in the earth; they will no longer be laughed at. They will laugh and rejoice because of God's presence and power operating in and through their lives"

My goodness what a glorious time the body of Christ his to look forward to, and the time is here for the fullness of this to manifest in every area of our lives.

## CHAPTER 17

# ENTERTAIN COVENANT PEOPLE

**Gen 26:30-31**

**30** And he made them a [formal] dinner, and they ate and drank.

In this chapter, the Angel explained to me that he must give me a gift. He said that it is a gift of the ability to receive the power of divine expansion. He said that this gift will allow me to receive all levels and dimensions of the kind of success and prosperity that God wants me to experience in the earth without being concerned about what people may think or say about it. He said that it should be noted that after Isaac realized the reason for King Abimelech and his friends visiting him, he invited them to spend the night at his home. He treated them with kindness before he made the covenant with them.

This gives us a look into Isaac's living conditions were lived and the grandeur of his dwelling. His home was of the level of opulence that could have a King and his friends as guest for a night. The Angel said that this is very important to receive, because a great part of the hundredfold manifestation is to translate individuals in the body of Christ to the level of living that they can entertain key persons as the kingdom of God advances in the earth realm.

Isaac invited King Abimelech and his friends to spend the night with him, and instructed his servants prepare a formal dinner prepared for them. Afterwards he had his servants to escort them to their respective rooms.

What is spiritually powerful about this is that these men had the opportunity to spend one night in the home of the laughter of God, the home of the one who the Lord was with, the home of the blessed of the Lord.

What an experience it must have been for these men, to eat and rest in that presence for an entire night. This is the level that the Kingdom of God is bringing into the lives of the body of Christ in this season though the hundredfold manifestation as the Angel pointed out. Many will be able to open their houses to persons coming to make covenant with them to protect their lives, families and businesses and future success and prosperity, because they will see the presence and power of the Lord manifested in our lives on a daily basis.

The Angel said that the body of Christ will receive favour in real estate, in the automotive industry and in financial gifts that will quickly change their lives in line with the demands of the Kingdom of God.

He then gave me some examples of persons who had actually experienced this in the scripture.

## ABRAHAM'S FAVOR

### Gen 23:13-18

**13** And he said to Ephron in the presence of the people of the land, But if you will give it, I beg of you, hear me. I will give you the price of the field; accept it from me, and I will bury my dead there.

**14** Ephron replied to Abraham, saying,

**15** My lord, listen to me. The land is worth 400 shekels of silver; what is that between you and me? So bury your dead.

**16** So Abraham listened to what Ephron said and acted upon it. He weighed to Ephron the silver which he had named in the hearing of the Hittites: 400 shekels of silver, according to the weights current among the merchants.

**17** So the field of Ephron in Machpelah, which was to the east of Mamre [Hebron] – the field and the cave which was in it, and all the trees that were in the field and in all its borders round about – was made over

**18** As a possession to Abraham in the presence of the Hittites, before all who went in at his city gate. AMP

In this account, Abraham's wife Sarah has died, and his desires to bury her in a mountain. The land however belongs to Ephron the Hittite. When Abraham approached him to purchase the land and enquired of its price, Ephron said that it was worth four hundred shekels of silver, and asked him, "What is four hundred shekels between them." In other words, he told Abraham that he could have it for free.

Now even though this was a very generous offer, Abraham was able to pay Ephron the full price for the field, and take it as a possession, and buried Sarah there.

## ELISHA'S FAVOR

### 2 Kings 5:26

**26** Elisha said to him, Did not my spirit go with you when the man turned from his chariot to meet you? Was it a time to accept money, garments, olive orchards, vineyards, sheep, oxen, menservants, and maidservants? AMP

Here the Prophet Elisha in correcting his servant Gehazi, after he had went after Naaman the Syrian whom Elisha had healed, and received two changes of garments and two thousand shekels of silver from him, Elisha reminded him of the level of favour that he receives at.

Elisha said that he receives money, clothing, land, business, livestock and both men and maid servants as gifts.

The Angel said that this level of favour is returning to the body of Christ during this new hundredfold season.

## POINT: MEET WITH KEY PEOPLE

The Angel said that in addition to the level of favour that's coming to the body of Christ, it will also be very important for believers to strategically make appointments to see the right people who may have the resources, connections and financial capacity to help further their ministries and created greater impact for the Kingdom of God.

He said that in the life and ministry of Jesus Christ, he had the wisdom of meeting with key persons through the word of wisdom and knowledge. This wisdom and knowledge would make him go and see certain people even though it wasn't the likeable thing to do in the public's eyes.

This as the Angel explained is a higher kind of ministry that must be mastered by the body of Christ as we advance into the level of ministry that will change the world and bring in synchronization with the will of God through the Kingdom of God.

To reveal this higher level of ministry, I was lead to read Luke 19:1-10 as an example.

## Luke 19:1-10

**1** AND [Jesus] entered Jericho and was passing through it.

**2** And there was a man called Zacchaeus, a chief tax collector, and [he was] rich.

**3** And he was trying to see Jesus, which One He was, but he could not on account of the crowd, because he was small in stature.

**4** So he ran on ahead and climbed up in a sycamore tree in order to see Him, for He was about to pass that way.

**5** And when Jesus reached the place, He looked up and said to him, Zacchaeus, hurry and come down; for I must stay at your house today.

**6** So he hurried and came down, and he received and welcomed Him joyfully.

**7** And when the people saw it, they all muttered among themselves and indignantly complained, He has gone in to be the guest of and lodge with a man who is devoted to sin and preeminently a sinner.

**8** So then Zacchaeus stood up and solemnly declared to the Lord, See, Lord, the half of my goods I [now] give [by way of restoration] to the poor, and if I have cheated anyone out of anything, I [now] restore four times as much.

**9** And Jesus said to him, Today is [Messianic and spiritual] salvation come to [all the members of] this household, since Zacchaeus too is a [real spiritual] son of Abraham;

**10** For the Son of Man came to seek and to save that which was lost. AMP

Jesus, while passing through Jericho used the gift of the word of knowledge to locate a rich tax collector named Zacchaeus. This man had climbed into a sycamore tree to see Jesus as he passed by, but he was in for the shock of his life. Jesus stopped directly under the sycamore tree and called him down telling him that he must stay at his house today. Notice that Jesus made the appointment to see Zacchaeus.

Zacchaeus must have been so shocked at this and probably wondered how this man could have known where I was and my name at the same time. However according to the scripture, Zacchaeus hurried and came down from the tree and received and welcomed Jesus joyfully. Zacchaeus' reception of Jesus was so important to the level of ministry that he was going to receive from Him because Jesus went there to reveal to Zacchaeus the problem of ANTI-COVENANT LIVING.

The Angel revealed that even though Zacchaeus was so hated by the masses, that Jesus himself came under their scrutiny for going to his house. Zacchaeus was living well, wealthy and was probably connected to the then Roman political hierarchy. However his influence and character among the masses was in a grave state. The people disliked him and considered him to be a chief sinner.

However, by the time Jesus had concluded his conversation with Zacchaeus, he was ready to change the lives of the poor around him and restore those who were extorted by him in the business realm with four times as much. Can you imagine the joy that he brought to the people in one day? Whatever Jesus said to him got him back on track with the covenant life of the oath of Abraham and living out his name.

The Angel asked me to find the meaning of Zacchaeus's name, and when I did, I was stunned, Zacchaeus means: pure; clean; just. His life was far from the true nature and character of his name.

This level of ministry by Jesus did not go down well with the people, but it is needed today. Jesus said that messianic and spiritual salvation had come to Zacchaeus' home since he is a seed or son of Abraham.

**Luke 19:9-10**

**9** And Jesus said to him, Today is [Messianic and spiritual] salvation come to [all the members of] this household, since Zacchaeus too is a [real spiritual] son of Abraham;

**10** For the Son of Man came to seek and to save that which was lost. AMP

This shows why Jesus had to go to Zacchaeus's house. The one to whom the oath of Abraham was made had to visit a spiritual son of Abraham to reconnect and activate him in the power of the oath of Abraham.

The Angel then sent forth a power electrical energy into my body and said, "It is here again, the Son of Man is seeking and saving that which was lost from the sons of Abraham, we are giving it back to them Hallelujah, Amen."

This experience changed the home of Zacchaeus forever, and in one day Jesus was able to restore this hated son of Abraham to having the dominion in Jericho. He brought great joy to families and individual by his amazing act that Jesus himself rejoiced at the manifestation.

He continued to reveal that the Lord will anoint individuals in this season who will be able to carry the level of presence and ability to meet and speak with individuals who are like Zacchaeus in nations of the world, who are unaware of their connection to Abraham, and who are to manifest this oath with power to sway the regions and nations in the direction of the Kingdom.

The Angel says that this higher level ministry around the world will change the very core of what the kingdom of God has been doing in recent times in the earth. The time to have the power and wisdom to meet with the right people and cause them to experience the presence and revelation of God is here. He will give supernatural covenant understanding to individuals, which will cause them to open their hearts to receive higher truth about their purpose and position in the earth that will activate them to bring about instant change in the lives of many in their respective regions and the world. Others will come to the ministers that receive this revelation seeking the way of the Lord, because I will speak to them.

There will come a new understanding in the minds of many ministers in the Body of Christ today because I have released it to them. They now know their place in the kingdom and in the nations of the world. They will not be afraid to entertain Kings, presidents, businessmen, royalty, governors, politicians, athletes and entertainer in this time. As they do this, much good will begin to come to nations and the poor in their lands will see the goodness of the Lord." There is a new divine level of influence that is here for the Body of Christ. We have to get back to covenant fulfilment living.

CHAPTER 18

# YOUR NEW DAY IS HERE

**Gen 26:31**

**31** And they rose up early in the morning and took oaths [with a curse] with one another; and Isaac sent them on their way and they departed from him in peace. AMP

As we entered into this phase of the visitation, the Angel continued to release more in-depth knowledge about the changes that had quickly occurred in Isaac's mind. He said that during the night of King Abimelech and his friends stayed at his home, Isaac began to truly realize the power and position he held in the earth.

Isaac, King Abimelech and his friend rose early in the morning and made the covenant with the oath, and Isaac sent them away in peace. The covenant was made with the rising of the sun, bringing in a new day in the lives of these four men, their families, their descendants and nations. A divine future was set. Isaac sent them on their way home in peace or settled in their relationship and the covenant they had made.

The Angel said, "Look at it, Isaac sent them away in peace, it wasn't how they sent him away from Gerar, but he became the man of peace in the earth."

He then said to me, "Remember I told you that what happened with Isaac must happen with Jesus Christ?" I replied, "Yes".

The he said to me to consider these scriptures...

**Acts 10:36**

**36** You know the contents of the message which He sent to Israel, announcing the good news (Gospel) of peace by Jesus Christ, Who is Lord of all — AMP

**Eph 2:15**

**15** By abolishing in His [own crucified] flesh the enmity [caused by] the Law with its decrees and ordinances [which He annulled]; that He from the two might create in Himself one new man [one new quality of humanity out of the two], so making peace. AMP

**Col 1:20**

**20** And God purposed that through (by the service, the intervention of) Him [the Son] all things should be completely reconciled back to Himself, whether on earth or in heaven, as through Him, [the Father] made peace by means of the blood of His cross. AMP

**John 14:27**

**27** Peace I leave with you; My [own] peace I now give and bequeath to you. Not as the world gives do I give to you. Do not let your hearts be troubled, neither let them be afraid. AMP

The Angel revealed that the key of the outcome of Jesus's purpose was to create peace on all levels and dimensions. Jesus Christ, like Isaac was in his day is the true man of peace. It is the Hebrew word *Shalom* which means peace, completeness, welfare, health, and the Greek *Eirene* meaning harmonious relationships.

The new day of God in the body of Christ will be a new day of peace creation in every area of life and its affairs. The Angel said that they will be released in great ways and waves to assist the children of God to see their current standing in life, and their situations all change rapidly for the better. He said that we will bring the healings, miracle and spiritual transition that are necessary to cause the peace that will be needed for the power of the Kingdom to flow in greater manifestations.

He said that they will cause dreams and visions to come to past, and end the resistance and restriction imposed on the body of Christ by satanic forces. The peace of God and his love will join together in a dazzling array of power and glory, breaking the powers of darkness once and for all for the body of Christ across the nations of the world.

## Point: GO TO THE NEXT LEVEL

### Gen 26:32-33

That same day Isaac's servants came and told him about the well they had dug, saying, We have found water!

**33** And he named [the well] Shibah; therefore the name of the city is Beersheba [well of the oath] to this day.

Coming into this aspect of the visitation, the Angel shared with me that at this point in his life; Isaac began to experience the life that was in synchronization with the revelation of his name, the laughter of God. Everything was manifesting according to plan and each new event was on time.

The same day that Isaac made the oath with King and his friends, his servants found a well. What are the odds of this happening on the same day that the oath was made? We have to understand that certain things will not be released or revealed in the earth until certain personal, spiritual and governmental covenants have been made in the earth again. The earth realm has to become a place of covenant and accountability again. The Angel said to me that at this point they were revealing new things to Isaac and his household. We were granting him and them divine assistance on another level.

When Isaac received the news of the well, he named it Shibah which means oath. As you recall in Genesis 21:31, Abraham came into the knowledge of the well at Beersheba through supernatural means, but now to Isaac's further joy, his servant has found him his own well at Beersheba.

With this find, Isaac began to construct a City there. With the two wells of oath in his possession, he began the process of expanding what his father Abraham started. The Hebrew word for city is Iyr, which means, a place guarded by waking or a watch. Isaac was building a City that was watched by two oaths, one made by his father and the other by himself with the same King.

The Angel said that there is a kind of laughter that hasn't been heard in the earth from the body of Christ, but it will take a greater level of manifestation to produce greater laughter in this season. This new season of the hundredfold will see more individual in the Body of Christ break barriers in every arena of life on this planet.

He said, "Do you not know that Jesus demands that his church becomes a barrier breaking, record breaking church, for this is what he meant when he said, that great works you shall do, because he goes to the Father."

**John 14:12**

**12** I assure you, most solemnly I tell you, if anyone steadfastly believes in Me, he will himself be able to do the things that I do; and he will do even greater things than these, because I go to the Father. AMP

## PROPHETIC WORD FROM THE ANGEL

"The Lord will pour out His Spirit mightily on the body of Christ for more to be done in this time; it will be the anointing and grace to break records handed to the children of the Kingdom, to do the seemingly impossible task in owning and building things that will leave the world in awe. It will be the time of great debt cancelation and acceleration in dominion living. We're flowing from glory to glory, possessing the power of the air, demonstration of power, showing forth signs and wonders and hidden wisdom such as never seen before, and you are to enforce this to the body of Christ."

## Point: THE DOUBLE IS YOURS

In continuing his revelation, the Angel Isaac began to emphasise the fact that Isaac naming the well Shibah or Sheba, meaning 'oath' was very prophetic. This city that he is building here became the place of two wells, and both wells were found supernaturally. There were now two oaths made in the same place, with the same King, with the same Lord watching over all.

Everything was doubled; Isaac was now the blessed of the Lord in the earth realm and the Lord increased him exponentially in all things. The Angel said that there must be a certain level of divine presence granted in order for the double to manifest itself, and that this level of presence will be released into the body of Christ in the season of the hundredfold.

He said that the double, like the hundredfold is a gift from God and not the result of hard work. The double where God is concerned isn't twice as much it is actually twice as much as it originally should've been.

In taking me to the scripture to explain his revelation, I was directed the two passages.

**Isa 61:7**

**7** Instead of your [former] shame you shall have a twofold recompense; instead of dishonor and reproach [your people] shall rejoice in their portion. Therefore in their land they shall possess double [what they had forfeited]; everlasting joy shall be theirs. AMP

**Zech 9:12**

**12** Return to the stronghold [of security and prosperity], you prisoners of hope; even today do I declare that I will restore double your former prosperity to you. AMP

The Angel said, "Note well that in each verse it is clear that what I said to you about the double is revealed here, and this is the kind of double that's coming to the body of Christ through this hundredfold manifestation."

CHAPTER 19

# WISDOM FOR MARRIAGE

In this final chapter, the Angel said to me, "This principle of wisdom for marriage is very important for individuals in the body of Christ who are contemplating it. They must begin to pray for wisdom in finding the correct partner, as the wrong partner can block blessing and fulfilment of divine purpose."

In the final verses of Genesis Chapter 26, reveals is serious situation that Isaac faced due to his son Esau's marital error.

**Gen 26:34-35**

**34** Now Esau was 40 years old when he took as wife Judith the daughter of Beeri the Hittite, and Basemath the daughter of Elon the Hittite.

**35** And they made life bitter and a grief of mind and spirit for Isaac and Rebekah [their parents-in-law].

The Angel continued explaining that it is very critical that the correct assessments, observances and questionings be done in order to come to a personal and spiritual realization of the individual that is showing interest or maybe to the person of interest.

In the text we see Esau one of the twins that the Lord gave to Isaac and his wife Rebecca, marrying two Hitite women. The word Hitite means broken and fearful. One of their names was Judith, meaning 'praise', the other Basemath, meaning 'perfume-confusion of death-desolation'. Brokenness and fear mixed with praise and confusion will never work out.

These two young ladies, according to the scripture, made life for Isaac and Rebecca bitter with grief of mind and spirit. They totally disrespected their Parents in Law at every opportunity they had. This is something that Esau should have put to a stop, but he allowed it to continue.

This was due to the fact that they did not understand the kind of family they were marrying into. They did not know, nor did they become acquainted with the blessing of the Lord or the will of God for the life of Esau or his father. They did not understand the life of faith or the blessing.

The Angel said, "Tell our people not to marry anyone who will not honour those with the blessing, and those who manifest that the can dishonour parents willfully." It takes a lifestyle of faith to live by the blessing of God."

In Genesis 24, Abraham seemed to have realized the spiritual and mental state of the women of the Canaanites, and made his servant Eliezer to swear not to allow his son Isaac to marry any of them.

**Gen 24:2-4**

**2** And Abraham said to the eldest servant of his house [Eliezer of Damascus], who ruled over all that he had, I beg of you, put your hand under my thigh; [Gen 15:2.]

**3** And you shall swear by the Lord, the God of heaven and earth, that you will not take a wife for my son from the daughters of the Canaanites, among whom I have settled,

**4** But you shall go to my country and to my relatives and take a wife for my son Isaac.

Abraham knew that it was very important to be happy in marriage and wanted the same for his son Isaac. He knew that a Canaanite woman would not have been a good choice. The name Canaan means: merchant; trader; or that humbles and subdues. Canaan is the grandson of Ham the son of Noah whom he had cursed. Abraham understood the importance of the purpose of Isaac in the earth, and knew that it was necessary for him to have someone in his life that would not be cantered on their own way or dishonour him and distract him. The behavior of Esau's wives was not befitting when compared to the behavior of Rebecca and Sarah.

# INTELLIGENCE IN MARRIAGE

## 1 Peter 3:6-7

**6** It was thus that Sarah obeyed Abraham [following his guidance and acknowledging his headship over her by] calling him lord (master, leader, authority). And you are now her true daughters if you do right and let nothing terrify you [not giving way to hysterical fears or letting anxieties unnerve you].

**7** In the same way you married men should live considerately with [your wives], with an intelligent recognition [of the marriage relation], honoring the woman as [physically] the weaker, but [realizing that you] are joint heirs of the grace (God's unmerited favor) of life, in order that your prayers may not be hindered and cut off. [Otherwise you cannot pray effectively.]

In explaining this vital key in the visitation, the Angel showed me that both the male and the female must seek to develop themselves in the proper manner, so that they can contribute purposefully and effectively to the marriage.

In the text, Sarah was mature enough to call Abraham her Lord and yield to his counsel, because Abraham was following the commands of God and walking by faith. He was a visionary.

The Apostle Peter explains that it is the responsibility of the man to have an intelligent recognition of the marriage covenant, honouring her physically weaker state, and realizing the position of being joint heirs of the grace of God, so that the prayers of the man will not be hindered.

He explains that the incorrect structure in marriage and become a blockage to the spiritual realm responding. So it become vital for men and women to grow in the true knowledge of what a marriage covenant is all about.

## THE APOSTLE PAUL ON MARRIAGE

### Eph 5:22-25

**22** Wives, be subject (be submissive and adapt yourselves) to your own husbands as [a service] to the Lord.

**23** For the husband is head of the wife as Christ is the Head of the church, Himself the Savior of [His] body.

**24** As the church is subject to Christ, so let wives also be subject in everything to their husbands.

**25** Husbands, love your wives, as Christ loved the church and gave Himself up for her, AMP

Here in the text the Apostle Paul beautifully reveals the two dimensions of ministry for both the husband and the wife in marriage. He says that the wife should be submissive and seek to adapt to the husband as a service to the Lord. This means that she should consider that the Lord has employed her to love and assist her husband.

The husband on the other hand is to love his wife as Christ loved the church and gave himself for her. This means that the husband should have a plan to help his wife evolve into the best version of herself, but doing what is necessary to himself on her behalf.

As you can see here like with the Apostle Peter, both the husband and the wife have separate and distinct element to bring into the marriage covenant in order to make in into a true marriage that will produce oneness.

The Angel said, "With the joy that will come with the manifestation of the hundredfold, the Lord wants us to be watchful and seek to know whether those we get involved with have a Minister or an influential person in their lives that they hold in high esteem. Do they honour someone or do they have a history of treating everyone around them with blatant disrespect? Do they have a history of sowing into anyone? Do they tithe? Do they love studying the word? Do they practice a praying lifestyle? What are their beliefs?

These are some to the critical questions and signs that you will have to ask and look for as you prepare yourself for marriage in this season. You have to look for the warning signs. Marriage must not be entered into unadvisedly. Seek godly counsel before you take that step.

The Body of Christ has been plagued with divorce, separation and all round failure of marriages because of the lack of honour and intelligence in the hearts of men and women. Ministers all over the world have had many setbacks and unhealthy situations to handle in the church because of the lack of honour in marriages. The Lord wants to make this a thing of the past in the Body of Christ today and this season of the hundredfold will play a major role in creating greater power in the hearts of individuals in the kingdom.

## JESUS'S POSITION ON MARRIAGE

### Matt 19:4-5

**4** He replied, Have you never read that He Who made them from the beginning made them male and female,

**5** And said, For this reason a man shall leave his father and mother and shall be united firmly (joined inseparably) to his wife, and the two shall become one flesh?

The Angel explained here that Jesus explained a great principle when he was asked about marriage. Jesus said that the man should join to his wife, meaning that it is his responsibility to create the system to foster a true connection to the woman. He further said that the tow should become one flesh, which means that they should evolve into something other, a bigger and brighter version that couldn't be produce in the state of singleness.

There is a great need today throughout the world for the understanding of marriage. Jesus makes it plain that God designed it for a male and female to become one. He makes it clear that becoming one is the purpose of God for the marriage covenant, and this must become the sole desire of every married couple.

# CONCLUSION

After visiting with me for seven consecutive nights, sharing this revelation with me, the presence ceased, but I was left with an amazing experience that changed my life, thinking and ministry for ever.

I am forever grateful to God for choosing me to share this revelation with and granting me the opportunity to be a blessing and an agent of change in the body of Christ today.

In his parting words, the Angel said, "Now go forth, release the Order of Protection upon the people, challenge them to sow, and we will be with you to help them receive the Hundredfold manifestation."

I know that the body of Christ around the world is about to experience an amazing day of God's goodness as he pours out the hundredfold into the lives of his children in this season and beyond.

I trust that as you have read this book that you would be inspired to believe God for his gift of the hundredfold manifesting in your life and lifting you to a new level and dimension of power and influence in every area of your life.

## ORDER OF PROTECTION PRAYER

I pray now that the Order of Divine Protection is released upon you, your family, church, ministry and business, and that any satanic or human forces that tries to touch you in any negative way, will be put to death.

I release divine assistance to help you achieve your hundredfold manifestation in this season in Jesus Name. Amen.

www.ingramcontent.com/pod-product-compliance
Lightning Source LLC
Chambersburg PA
CBHW030252130626
46549CB00002B/495

* 9 7 8 1 9 6 5 6 3 2 9 2 5 *